THE STORY
OF MY MISFORTUNES

The Story of My Misfortunes

THE AUTOBIOGRAPHY OF
PETER ABÉLARD

TRANSLATED BY
HENRY ADAMS BELLOWS

INTRODUCTION BY
RALPH ADAMS CRAM

MACMILLAN PUBLISHING CO., INC.
NEW YORK
COLLIER MACMILLAN PUBLISHERS
LONDON

Facsimile of the original manuscript

INTRODUCTION

THE "Historia Calamitatum" of Peter Abélard is one of those human documents, out of the very heart of the Middle Ages, that illuminates by the glow of its ardour a shadowy period that has been made even more dusky and incomprehensible by unsympathetic commentators and the ill-digested matter of "source-books." Like the "Confessions" of St. Augustine it is an authentic revelation of personality and, like the latter, it seems to show how unchangeable is man, how consistent unto himself whether he is of the sixth century or the twelfth—or indeed of the twentieth century. "Evolution" may change the flora and fauna of the world, or modify its physical forms, but man is always the same and the unrolling of the centuries affects him not at all. If we can assume the vivid personality, the enormous intellectual power and the clear, keen mentality of Abélard and his contemporaries and immediate successors, there is no reason why "The Story of My Misfortunes" should not have been written within the last decade.

They are large assumptions, for this is not a period in world-history when the informing energy of life expresses itself through such qualities, whereas the twelfth century was of precisely this nature. The antecedent hundred years had seen the recovery from the barbarism that engulfed Western Europe after the fall of Rome, and the generation of those vital forces that for two centuries were to infuse society with a vigour almost unexampled in its potency and in the things it brought to pass. The parabolic curve that describes the trajectory of Mediaevalism was then emergent out of "chaos and old night" and Abélard and his opponent, St. Bernard, rode high on the mounting force in its swift and almost violent ascent.

Pierre du Pallet, yclept Abélard, was born in 1079 and died in 1142, and his life precisely covers the period of the birth, development and perfecting of that Gothic style of architecture which is one of the great exemplars of the period. Actually, the Norman development occupied the years from 1050 to 1125 while the initiating and determining of Gothic consumed only fifteen years, from Bury, begun in 1125, to Saint-Denis, the work of Abbot Suger, the friend and partisan of Abélard, in 1140. It was the time of the Crusades, of the founding and development of schools and universities, of the invention or recovery of great arts, of the growth of music, poetry and romance. It was the age of great kings and knights and leaders of all kinds, but above all it was the epoch of a new philosophy, refounded on the newly revealed corner stones of Plato and Aristotle, but with a new content, a new impulse and a new method inspired by Christianity.

All these things, philosophy, art, personality, character, were the product of the time, which, in its definiteness and consistency, stands apart from all other epochs in history. The social system was that of feudalism, a scheme of reciprocal duties, privileges and obligations as between man and man that has never been excelled by any other system that society has developed as its own method of operation. As Dr. De Wulf has said in his illuminating book "Philosophy and Civilization in the Middle Ages" (a volume that should be read by any one who wishes rightly to understand the spirit and quality of Mediaevalism), "the feudal sentiment *par excellence* . . . is the sentiment of the value and dignity of the individual man. The feudal man lived as a free man; he was master in his own house; he sought his end in himself; he was—and this is a scholastic expression,—*propter seipsum existens:* all feudal obligations were founded upon respect for personality and the given word."

Of course this admirable scheme of society with its guild system of industry, its absence of usury in any form and its just sense of comparative values, was shot through and through with religion both in faith and practice. Catholicism was universally and implicitly accepted. Monasticism had redeemed Europe from barbarism and Cluny had freed the Church from the yoke of German imperialism. This unity and immanence of religion gave a consistency to society otherwise unobtainable, and poured its vitality into every form of human thought and action.

It was Catholicism and the spirit of feudalism that preserved men from the dangers inherent in the immense individualism of the time. With this powerful and penetrating coördinating force men were safe to go about as far as they liked in the line of individuality, whereas to-day, for example, the unifying force of a common and vital religion being absent and nothing having been offered to take its place, the result of a similar tendency is egotism and anarchy. These things happened in the end in the case of Mediaevalism when the power and the influence of religion once began to weaken, and the Renaissance and Reformation dissolved the fabric of a unified society. Thereafter it became necessary to bring some order out of the spiritual, intellectual and physical chaos through the application of arbitrary force, and so came absolutism in government, the tyranny of the new intellectualism, the Catholic Inquisition and the Puritan Theocracy.

In the twelfth and thirteenth centuries, however, the balance is justly preserved, though it was but an unstable equilibrium, and therefore during the time of Abélard we find the widest diversity of speculation and freedom of thought which continue unhampered for more than a hundred years. The mystical school of the Abbey of St. Victor in Paris follows one line (perhaps the most nearly right of all though it was submerged by the intellectual force and vivacity of the Scholastics) with Hugh of St. Victor as its greatest exponent. The Franciscans and

Dominicans each possessed great schools of philosophy and dogmatic theology, and in addition there were a dozen individual lines of speculation, each vitalized by some one personality, daring, original, enthusiastic. This prodigious mental and spiritual activity was largely fostered by the schools, colleges and universities that had suddenly appeared all over Europe. Never was such activity along educational lines. Almost every cathedral had its school, and many of the abbeys as well, as for example, in France alone, Cluny, Citeaux and Bec, St. Martin of Tours, Laon, Chartres, Rheims and Paris. To these schools students poured in from all over the world in numbers mounting to many thousands for such as Paris for example, and the mutual rivalries were intense and sometimes disorderly. Groups of students would choose their own masters and follow them from place to place, even subjecting them to discipline if in their opinion they did not live up to the intellectual mark they had set as their standard. As there was not only one religion and one social system, but one universal language as well, this gathering from all the four quarters of Europe was perfectly possible, and had much to do with the maintenance of that unity which marked society for three centuries.

At the time of Abélard the schools of Chartres and Paris were at the height of their fame and power. Fulbert, Bernard and Thierry, all of Chartres, had fixed its fame for a long period, and at Paris Hugh and Richard of St. Victor and William of Champeaux were names to conjure with, while Anselm of Laon, Adelard of Bath, Alan of Lille, John of Salisbury, Peter Lombard, were all from time to time students or teachers in one of the schools of the Cathedral, the Abbey of St. Victor or Ste. Geneviève.

Earlier in the Middle Ages the identity of theology and philosophy had been proclaimed, following the Neo-Platonic and Augustinian theory, and the latter (cf. Peter Damien and Duns Scotus Eriugena) was even reduced to a position that made it no more than the obedient handmaid of theology. In the eleventh century however, St. Anselm had drawn a clear distinction between faith and reason, and thereafter theology and philosophy were generally accepted as individual but allied sciences, both serving as lines of approach to truth but differing in their method. Truth was one and therefore there could be no conflict between the conclusions reached after different fashions. In the twelfth century Peter of Blois led a certain group called "rigourists" who still looked askance at philosophy, or rather at the intellectual methods by which it proceeded, and they were inclined to condemn it as "the devil's art," but they were on the losing side and John of Salisbury, Alan of Lille, Gilbert de la Porrée and Hugh of St. Victor prevailed in their contention that philosophers were *"humanae videlicet sapientiae amatores,"* while theologians were *"divinae scripturae doctores."*

Cardinal Mercier, himself the greatest contemporary

exponent of Scholastic philosophy, defines philosophy as "the science of the totality of things." The twelfth century was a time when men were striving to see phenomena in this sense and established a great rational synthesis that should yet be in full conformity with the dogmatic theology of revealed religion. Abélard was one of the most enthusiastic and daring of these Mediaeval thinkers, and it is not surprising that he should have found himself at issue not only with the duller type of theologians but with his philosophical peers themselves. He was an intellectual force of the first magnitude and a master of dialectic; he was also an egotist through and through, and a man of strong passions. He would and did use his logical faculty and his mastery of dialectic to justify his own desires, whether these were for carnal satisfaction or the maintenance of an original intellectual concept. It was precisely this danger that aroused the fears of the "rigourists" and in the light of succeeding events in the domain of intellectualism it is impossible to deny that there was some justification for their gloomy apprehensions. In St. Thomas Aquinas this intellectualizing process marked its highest point and beyond there was no margin of safety. He himself did not overstep the verge of danger, but after him this limit was overpassed. The perfect balance between mind and spirit was achieved by Hugh of St. Victor, but afterwards the severance began and on the one side was the unwholesome hyperspiritualization of the Rhenish mystics, on the other the false intellectualism of Descartes, Kant and the entire modern school of materialistic philosophy. It was the clear prevision of this inevitable issue that made of St. Bernard not only an implacable opponent of Abélard but of the whole system of Scholasticism as well. For a time he was victorious. Abélard was silenced and the mysticism of the Victorines triumphed, only to be superseded fifty years later when the two great orders, Dominican and Franciscan, produced their triumphant protagonists of intellectualism, Alexander Hales and Albertus Magnus, and finally the greatest pure intellect of all time, St. Thomas Aquinas. St. Bernard, St. Francis of Assisi, the Victorines, maintained that after all, as Henri Bergson was to say, seven hundred years later, "the mind of man by its very nature is incapable of apprehending reality," and that therefore faith is better than reason. Lord Bacon came to the same conclusion when he wrote "Let men please themselves as they will in admiring and almost adoring the human kind, this is certain; that, as an uneven mirrour distorts the rays of objects according to its own figure and section, so the mind . . cannot be trusted." And Hugh of St. Victor himself, had written, even in the days of Abélard: "There was a certain wisdom that seemed such to them that knew not the true wisdom. The world found it and began to be puffed up, thinking itself great in this. Confiding in its wisdom it became presumptuous and boasted it would attain the highest wisdom. And it made itself a

[VIII]

ladder of the face of creation. . . . Then those things which were seen were known and there were other things which were not known; and through those which were manifest they expected to reach those that were hidden. And they stumbled and fell into the falsehoods of their own imagining . . . So God made foolish the wisdom of this world, and He pointed out another wisdom, which seemed foolishness and was not. For it preached Christ crucified, in order that truth might be sought in humility. But the world despised it, wishing to contemplate the works of God, which He had made a source of wonder, and it did not wish to venerate what He had set for imitation, neither did it look to its own disease, seeking medicine in piety; but presuming on a false health, it gave itself over with vain curiosity to the study of alien things."

These considerations troubled Abélard not at all. He was conscious of a mind of singular acuteness and a tongue of parts, both of which would do whatever he willed. Beneath all the tumultuous talk of Paris, when he first arrived there, lay the great and unsolved problem of Universals and this he promptly made his own, rushing in where others feared to tread. William of Champeaux had rested on a Platonic basis, Abélard assumed that of Aristotle, and the clash began. It is not a lucid subject, but the best abstract may be found in Chapter XIV of Henry Adams' "Mont-Saint-Michel and Chartres" while this and the two succeeding chapters give the most luminous and vivacious account of the principles at issue in this most vital of intellectual feuds.

"According to the latest authorities, the doctrine of universals which convulsed the schools of the twelfth century has never received an adequate answer. What is a species? what is a genus or a family or an order? More or less convenient terms of classification, about which the twelfth century cared very little, while it cared deeply about the essence of classes! Science has become too complex to affirm the existence of universal truths, but it strives for nothing else, and disputes the problem, within its own limits, almost as earnestly as in the twelfth century, when the whole field of human and superhuman activity was shut between these barriers of substance, universals, and particulars. Little has changed except the vocabulary and the method. The schools knew that their society hung for life on the demonstration that God, the ultimate universal, was a reality, out of which all other universal truths or realities sprang. Truth was a real thing, outside of human experience. The schools of Paris talked and thought of nothing else. John of Salisbury, who attended Abélard's lectures about 1136, and became Bishop of Chartres in 1176, seems to have been more surprised than we need be at the intensity of the emotion. 'One never gets away from this question,' he said. 'From whatever point a discussion starts, it is always led back and attached to that. It is the madness of Rufus about Naevia; "He thinks of nothing else; talks of nothing else, and if Naevia did not exist, Rufus would be dumb." '

. . . "In these scholastic tournaments the two champions started from opposite points:—one from the ultimate substance, God,—the universal, the ideal, the type;—the other from the individual, Socrates, the concrete, the observed fact of experience, the object of sensual perception. The first champion—William in this instance—assumed that the universal was a real thing; and for that reason he was called a realist. His opponent —Abélard—held that the universal was only nominally real; and on that account he was called a nominalist. Truth, virtue, humanity, exist as units and realities, said William. Truth, replied Abélard, is only the sum of all possible facts that are true, as humanity is the sum of all actual human beings. The ideal bed is a form, made by God, said Plato. The ideal bed is a name, imagined by ourselves, said Aristotle. 'I start from the universe,' said William. 'I start from the atom,' said Abélard; and, once having started, they necessarily came into collision at some point between the two."

In this "Story of My Misfortunes" Abélard gives his own account of the triumphant manner in which he confounded his master, William, but as Henry Adams says, "We should be more credulous than twelfth-century monks, if we believed, on Abélard's word in 1135, that in 1110 he had driven out of the schools the most accomplished dialectician of the age by an objection so familiar

[XI]

that no other dialectician was ever silenced by it—whatever may have been the case with theologians—and so obvious that it could not have troubled a scholar of fifteen. William stated a selected doctrine as old as Plato; Abélard interposed an objection as old as Aristotle. Probably Plato and Aristotle had received the question and answer from philosophers ten thousand years older than themselves. Certainly the whole of philosophy has always been involved in this dispute."

So began the battle of the schools with all its more than military strategy and tactics, and in the end it was a drawn battle, in spite of its marvels of intellectual heroism and dialectical sublety. Says Henry Adams again:—

"In every age man has been apt to dream uneasily, rolling from side to side, beating against imaginary bars, unless, tired out, he has sunk into indifference or scepticism. Religious minds prefer scepticism. The true saint is a profound sceptic; a total disbeliever in human reason, who has more than once joined hands on this ground with some who were at best sinners. Bernard was a total disbeliever in Scholasticism; so was Voltaire. Bernard brought the society of his time to share his scepticism, but could give the society no other intellectual amusement to relieve its restlessness. His crusade failed; his ascetic enthusiasm faded; God came no nearer. If there was in all France, between 1140 and 1200, a more typical Englishman of the future Church of England type than

John of Salisbury, he has left no trace; and John wrote a description of his time which makes a picturesque contrast with the picture painted by Abélard, his old master, of the century at its beginning. John weighed Abélard and the schools against Bernard and the cloister, and coolly concluded that the way to truth led rather through Citeaux, which brought him to Chartres as Bishop in 1176, and to a mild scepticism in faith. 'I prefer to doubt' he said, 'rather than rashly define what is hidden.' The battle with the schools had then resulted only in creating three kinds of sceptics:—the disbelievers in human reason; the passive agnostics; and the sceptics proper, who would have been atheists had they dared. The first class was represented by the School of St. Victor; the second by John of Salisbury himself; the third, by a class of schoolmen whom he called Cornificii, as though they made a practice of inventing horns of dilemma on which to fix their opponents; as, for example, they asked whether a pig which was led to market was led by the man or the cord. One asks instantly: What cord?— Whether Grace, for instance, or Free Will?

"Bishop John used the science he had learned in the school only to reach the conclusion that, if philosophy were a science at all, its best practical use was to teach charity—love. Even the early, superficial debates of the schools, in 1100-50, had so exhausted the subject that the most intelligent men saw how little was to be gained by pursuing further those lines of thought. The twelfth

[XIII]

century had already reached the point where the seventeenth century stood when Descartes renewed the attempt to give a solid, philosophical basis for deism by his celebrated '*Cogito, ergo sum.*' Although that ultimate fact seemed new to Europe when Descartes revived it as the starting-point of his demonstration, it was as old and familiar as St. Augustine to the twelfth century, and as little conclusive as any other assumption of the Ego or the Non-Ego. The schools argued, according to their tastes, from unity to multiplicity, or from multiplicity to unity; but what they wanted was to connect the two. They tried realism and found that it led to pantheism. They tried nominalism and found that it ended in materialism. They attempted a compromise in conceptualism which begged the whole question. Then they lay down, exhausted. In the seventeenth century the same violent struggle broke out again, and wrung from Pascal the famous outcry of despair in which the French language rose, perhaps for the last time, to the grand style of the twelfth century. To the twelfth century it belongs; to the century of faith and simplicity; not to the mathematical certainties of Descartes and Leibnitz and Newton, or to the mathematical abstractions of Spinoza. Descartes had proclaimed his famous conceptual proof of God: 'I am conscious of myself, and must exist; I am conscious of God and He must exist.' Pascal wearily replied that it was not God he doubted, but logic. He was tortured by the impossibility of rejecting man's reason by reason; unconsciously sceptical, he forced himself to disbelieve in himself rather than admit a doubt of God. Man had tried to prove God, and had failed: 'The metaphysical proofs of God are so remote (*éloignées*) from the reasoning of men, and so contradictory (*impliquées*, far-fetched) that they made little impression; and even if they served to convince some people, it would only be during the instant that they see the demonstration; an hour afterwards they fear to have deceived themselves.' "

Abélard was always, as he has been called, a scholastic adventurer, a philosophical and theological freelance, and it was after the Calamity that he followed those courses that resulted finally in his silencing and his obscure death. It is almost impossible for us of modern times to understand the violence of partisanship aroused by his actions and published words that centre apparently around the placing of the hermitage he had made for himself under the patronage of the third Person of the Trinity, the Paraclete, the Spirit of love and compassion and consolation, and the consequent arguments by which he justified himself. To us it seems that he was only trying to exalt the power of the Holy Spirit, a pious action at the least, but to the episcopal and monastic conservators of the faith he seems to have been guilty of trying to rationalize an unsolvable mystery, to find an intellectual solution forbidden to man. In some obscure way the question seems to be involved in that other of

[xv]

the function of the Blessed Virgin as the fount of mercy and compassion, and at this time when the cult of the Mother of God had reached its highest point of potency and poignancy anything of the sort seemed intolerable.

For a time the affairs of Abélard prospered: Abbot Suger of Saint-Denis was his defender, and he enjoyed the favor of the Pope and the King. He was made an abbot and his influence spread in every direction. In 1137 the King died and conditions at Rome changed so that St. Bernard became almost Pope and King in his own person. Within a year he proceeded against Abélard; his "Theology" was condemned at a council of Sens, this judgment was confirmed by the Pope, and the penalty of silence was imposed on the author—probably the most severe punishment he could be called upon to endure. As a matter of fact it was fatal to him. He started forthwith for Rome but stopped at the Abbey of Cluny in the company of its Abbot, Peter the Venerable, "the most amiable figure of the twelfth century," and no very devoted admirer of St. Bernard, to whom, as a matter of fact, he had once written, "You perform all the difficult religious duties; you fast, you watch, you suffer; but you will not endure the easy ones—you do not love." Here he found two years of peace after his troubled life, dying in the full communion of the Church on 21 April, 1142.

The problems of philosophy and theology that were so vital in the Middle Ages interest us no more, even when they are less obscure than those so rife in the twelfth century, but the problem of human love is always new and so it is not perhaps surprising that the abiding interest concerns itself with Abélard's relationship with Héloïse. So far as he is concerned it is not a very savoury matter. He deliberately seduced a pupil, a beautiful girl entrusted to him by her uncle, a simple-minded old canon of the Cathedral of Paris, under whose roof he ensconced himself by false pretences and with the full intention of gaining the niece for himself. Abélard seems to have exercised an irresistible fascination for men and women alike, and his plot succeeded to admiration. Stricken by a belated remorse, he finally married Héloïse against her unselfish protests and partly to legitimatize his unborn child, and shortly after he was surprised and overpowered by emissaries of Canon Fulbert and subjected to irreparable mutilation. He tells the story with perfect frankness and with hardly more than formal expressions of compunction, and thereafter follows the narrative of their separation, he to a monastery, she to a convent, and of his care for her during her conventual life, or at least for that part of it that had passed before the "History" was written. Through the whole story it is Héloïse who shines brightly as a curiously beautiful personality, unselfish, self-sacrificing, and almost virginal in her purity in spite of her fault. One has for her only sympathy and affection whereas it is difficult to feel either for Abélard in spite of his belated efforts at rectifying his own sin and his life-long devotion to his solitary wife in her hidden cloister.

The whole story was instantly known, Abélard's assailants were punished in kind, and he himself shortly resumed his work of lecturing on philosophy and, a little later, on theology. Apparently his reputation did not suffer in the least, nor did hers; in fact her piety became almost a by-word and his fame as a great teacher increased by leaps and bounds: neither his offence nor its punishment seemed to bring lasting discredit. This fact, which seems strange to us, does not imply a lack of moral sense in the community but rather the prevalence of standards alien to our own. It is only since the advent of Puritanism that sexual sins have been placed at the head of the whole category. During the Middle Ages, as always under Christianity, the most deadly sins were pride, covetousness, slander and anger. These implied inherent moral depravity, but "illicit" love was love outside the law of man, and did not of necessity and always involve moral guilt. Christ was Himself very gentle and compassionate with the sins of the flesh but relentless in the case of the greater sins of the spirit. Puritanism overturned the balance of things, and by concentrating its condemnation on sexual derelictions became blind to the greater sins of pride, avarice and anger. We have inherited the prejudice without acquiring the abstention, but the Middle Ages had a clearer sense of comparative values and they could forgive, or even ignore, the sin of Abélard and Héloïse when they could less easily excuse the sin of spiritual pride or deliberate cruelty. Moreover, these same Middle Ages believed very earnestly in the Divine forgiveness of sins for which there had been real repentance and honest effort at amendment. Abélard and Héloïse had been grievously punished, he himself had made every reparation that was possible, his penitence was charitably assumed, and therefore it was not for society to condemn what God would mercifully forgive.

The twelfth and thirteenth centuries were not an age of moral laxity; ideals and standards and conduct were immeasurably higher than they had been for five hundred years, higher than they were to be in the centuries that followed the crest of Mediaevalism. It was however a time of enormous vitality, of throbbing energy that was constantly bursting its bounds, and as well a time of personal liberty and freedom of action that would seem strange indeed to us in these days of endless legal restraint and inhibitions mitigated by revolt. There were few formal laws but there was *Custom* which was a sovereign law in itself, and above all there was the moral law of the Church, establishing its great fundamental principles but leaving details to the working out of life itself. Behind the sin of Abélard lay his intolerable spiritual pride, his selfishness and his egotism, qualities that society at large did not recognize because of their devotion to his engaging personality and their admiration for his dazzling intellectual gifts. Their idol had sinned, he had been savagely punished, he had repented; that was all there was about it and the question was at an end.

In reading the Historia Calamitatum there is one consideration that suggests itself that is subject for serious thought. Written as it was some years after the great tragedy of his life, it gives a portrait that somehow seems out of focus. We know that during his early years in Paris Abélard was a bold and daring champion in the lists of dialectic; brilliant, persuasive, masculine to a degree; yet this self-portrait is of a man timid, suspicious, frightened of realities, shadows, possibilities. He is in abject terror of councils, hidden enemies, even of his life. The tone is querulous, even peevish at times, and always the egotism and the pride persist, while he seems driven by the whip of desire for intellectual adventure into places where he shrinks from defending himself, or is unable to do so. The antithesis is complete and one is driven to believe that the terrible mutilation to which he had been subjected had broken down his personality and left him in all things less than man. His narrative is full of accusations against all manner of people, but it is not necessary to take all these literally, for it is evident that his natural egotism, overlaid by the circumstances of his calamity, produced an almost pathological condition wherein suspicions became to him realities and terrors established facts.

It is doubtful if Abélard should be ranked very high

in the list of Mediaeval philosophers. He was more a dialectician than a creative force, and until the development of the episode with Héloïse he seems to have cared primarily for the excitement of debate, with small regard for the value of the subjects under discussion. As an intellectualist he had much to do with the subsequent abandonment of Plato in favour of Aristotle that was a mark of pure scholasticism, while the brilliancy of his dialectical method became a model for future generations. After the Calamity he turned from philosophy to theology and ethics and here he reveals qualities of nobility not evident before. Particularly does he insist upon the fact that it is the subjective intention that determines the moral value of human actions even if it does not change their essential character.

The story of this philosophical soldier of fortune is a romance from beginning to end, a poignant human drama shot through with passion, adventure, pathos and tragedy. In a sense it is an epitome of the earlier Middle Ages and through it shines the bright light of an era of fervid living, of exciting adventure, of phenomenal intellectual force and of large and comprehensive liberty. As a single episode of passion it is not particularly distinguished except for the appealing personality of Héloïse; as a phase in the development of Christian philosophy it is of only secondary value. United in one, the two factors achieve a brilliant dramatic unity that has made the story of Abélard and Héloïse immortal.

THE STORY
OF MY MISFORTUNES

FOREWORD

OFTEN the hearts of men and women are stirred, as likewise they are soothed in their sorrows, more by example than by words. And therefore, because I too have known some consolation from speech had with one who was a witness thereof, am I now minded to write of the sufferings which have sprung out of my misfortunes, for the eyes of one who, though absent, is of himself ever a consoler. This I do so that, in comparing your sorrows with mine, you may discover that yours are in truth nought, or at the most but of small account, and so shall you come to bear them more easily.

CHAPTER I

OF THE BIRTHPLACE OF PIERRE ABÉLARD
AND OF HIS PARENTS

KNOW, then, that I am come from a certain town which was built on the way into lesser Brittany, distant some eight miles, as I think, eastward from the city of Nantes, and in its own tongue called Palets. Such is the nature of that country, or, it may be, of them who dwell there—for in truth they are quick in fancy—that my mind bent itself easily to the study of letters. Yet more, I had a father who had won some smattering of letters before he had girded on the soldier's belt. And so it came about that long afterwards his love thereof was so strong that he saw to it that each son of his should be taught in letters even earlier than in the management of arms. Thus indeed did it come to pass. And because I was his first born, and for that reason the more dear to him, he sought with double diligence to have me wisely taught. For my part, the more I went forward in the study of letters, and ever more easily, the greater became the ardour of my devotion to them, until in truth I was so enthralled by my passion for learning that, gladly leaving to my brothers the pomp of glory in arms, the right of heritage and all the honours that should have been mine as the eldest born, I fled utterly from the court of Mars that I might win learning in the bosom of Minerva. And since I found the armory of logical reasoning more

[1]

dot Wur

lost learning
Goddess of wisdom

to my liking than the other forms of philosophy, I exchanged all other weapons for these, and to the prizes of victory in war I preferred the battle of minds in disputation. Thenceforth, journeying through many provinces, and debating as I went, going whithersoever I heard that the study of my chosen art most flourished, I became such an one as the Peripatetics.

teaching (learn

Trying to take logic and apply it to Christianity

Peripatetics school of Philosophy · Aristotle
walk up & down
the path
learning by talking while you walk back & forth

[2]

CHAPTER II

Of the Persecution He Had from His Master
William of Champeaux—Of His Adventures
at Melun, at Corbeil and at Paris—Of
His Withdrawal from the City of the
Parisians to Melun, and His Re-
turn to Mont Ste. Geneviève
—Of His Journey to His
Old Home

I CAME at length to Paris, where above all in those
days the art of dialectics was most flourishing, and
there did I meet William of Champeaux, my teacher, a
man most distinguished in his science both by his renown
and by his true merit. With him I remained for some
time, at first indeed well liked of him; but later I brought
him great grief, because I undertook to refute certain
of his opinions, not infrequently attacking him in disputation, and now and then in these debates I was
adjudged victor. Now this, to those among my fellow
students who were ranked foremost, seemed all the more
insufferable because of my youth and the brief duration
of my studies.

Out of this sprang the beginning of my misfortunes,
which have followed me even to the present day; the
more widely my fame was spread abroad, the more bitter was the envy that was kindled against me. It was
given out that I, presuming on my gifts far beyond the

warranty of my youth, was aspiring despite my tender years to the leadership of a school; nay, more, that I was making ready the very place in which I would undertake this task, the place being none other than the castle of Melun, at that time a royal seat. My teacher himself had some foreknowledge of this, and tried to remove my school as far as possible from his own. Working in secret, he sought in every way he could before I left his following to bring to nought the school I had planned and the place I had chosen for it. Since, however, in that very place he had many rivals, and some of them men of influence among the great ones of the land, relying on their aid I won to the fulfillment of my wish; the support of many was secured for me by reason of his own unconcealed envy. From this small inception of my school, my fame in the art of dialectics began to spread abroad, so that little by little the renown, not alone of those who had been my fellow students, but of our very teacher himself, grew dim and was like to die out altogether. Thus it came about that, still more confident in myself, I moved my school as soon as I well might to the castle of Corbeil, which is hard by the city of Paris, for there I knew there would be given more frequent chance for my assaults in our battle of disputation.

No long time thereafter I was smitten with a grievous illness, brought upon me by my immoderate zeal for study. This illness forced me to turn homeward to my native province, and thus for some years I was as if cut off from France. And yet, for that very reason, I was sought out all the more eagerly by those whose hearts were troubled by the lore of dialectics. But after a few years had passed, and I was whole again from my sickness, I learned that my teacher, that same William Archdeacon of Paris, had changed his former garb and joined an order of the regular clergy. This he had done, or so men said, in order that he might be deemed more deeply religious, and so might be elevated to a loftier rank in the prelacy, a thing which, in truth, very soon came to pass, for he was made bishop of Châlons. Nevertheless, the garb he had donned by reason of his conversion did nought to keep him away either from the city of Paris or from his wonted study of philosophy; and in the very monastery wherein he had shut himself up for the sake of religion he straightway set to teaching again after the same fashion as before.

To him did I return, for I was eager to learn more of rhetoric from his lips; and in the course of our many arguments on various matters, I compelled him by most potent reasoning first to alter his former opinion on the subject of the universals, and finally to abandon it altogether. Now, the basis of this old concept of his regarding the reality of universal ideas was that the same quality formed the essence alike of the abstract whole and of the individuals which were its parts: in other words, that there could be no essential differences among these individuals, all being alike save for such variety as might grow out of the many accidents of existence. Thereafter, however, he corrected this opinion, no longer maintaining that the same quality was the essence of all things, but that, rather, it manifested itself in them through diverse ways. This problem of universals is ever the most vexed one among logicians, to such a degree, indeed, that even Porphyry, writing in his "Isagoge" regarding universals, dared not attempt a final pronouncement thereon, saying rather: "This is the deepest of all problems of its kind." Wherefore it followed that when William had first revised and then finally abandoned altogether his views on this one subject, his lecturing sank into such a state of negligent reasoning that it could scarce be called lecturing on the science of dialectics at all; it was as if all his science had been bound up in this one question of the nature of universals.

Thus it came about that my teaching won such strength and authority that even those who before had clung most vehemently to my former master, and most bitterly attacked my doctrines, now flocked to my school. The very man who had succeeded to my master's chair in the Paris school offered me his post, in order that he might put himself under my tutelage along with all the rest, and this in the very place where of old his master and mine had reigned. And when, in so short a time, my master saw me directing the study of dialectics there, it is not easy to find words to tell with what envy he was consumed or with what pain he was tormented. He could not long, in truth, bear the anguish of what he felt to be his wrongs, and shrewdly he attacked me that he might drive me forth. And because there was nought in my conduct whereby he could come at me openly, he tried to steal away the school by launching the vilest calumnies against him who had yielded his post to me, and by putting in his place a certain rival of mine. So then I returned to Melun, and set up my school there as before; and the more openly his envy pursued me, the greater was the authority it conferred upon me. Even so held the poet: "Jealousy aims at the peaks; the winds storm the loftiest summits." (Ovid: "Remedy for Love," I, 369.)

Not long thereafter, when William became aware of the fact that almost all his students were holding grave doubts as to his religion, and were whispering earnestly among themselves about his conversion, deeming that he had by no means abandoned this world, he withdrew himself and his brotherhood, together with his students, to a certain estate far distant from the city. Forthwith I returned from Melun to Paris, hoping for peace from him in the future. But since, as I have said, he had caused my place to be occupied by a rival of mine, I pitched the camp, as it were, of my school outside the city on Mont Ste. Geneviève. Thus I was as one laying siege to him who had taken possession of my post. No sooner had my master heard of this than he brazenly returned post haste to the city, bringing back with him such students as he could, and reinstating his brotherhood in their former monastery, much as if he would free his soldiery, whom he had deserted, from my blockade. In truth, though, if it was his purpose to bring them succour, he did nought but hurt them. Before that time my rival had indeed had a certain number of students, of one sort and another, chiefly by reason of his lectures on Priscian, in which he was considered of great authority. After our master had returned, however, he lost nearly all of these followers, and thus was compelled to give up the direction of the school. Not long thereafter, apparently despairing further of worldly fame, he was converted to the monastic life.

Following the return of our master to the city, the combats in disputation which my scholars waged both with him himself and with his pupils, and the successes which fortune gave to us, and above all to me, in these wars, you have long since learned of through your own experience. The boast of Ajax, though I speak it more temperately, I still am bold enough to make:

". . . if fain you would learn now
How victory crowned the battle, by him was
I never vanquished."
(Ovid, "Metamorphoses," XIII, 89.)

But even were I to be silent, the fact proclaims itself, and its outcome reveals the truth regarding it.

While these things were happening, it became needful for me again to repair to my old home, by reason of my dear mother, Lucia, for after the conversion of my father, Berengarius, to the monastic life, she so ordered her affairs as to do likewise. When all this had been completed, I returned to France, above all in order that I might study theology, since now my oft-mentioned teacher, William, was active in the episcopate of Châlons. In this field of learning Anselm of Laon, who was his teacher therein, had for long years enjoyed the greatest renown.

CHAPTER III

OF HOW HE CAME TO LAON TO SEEK ANSELM
AS TEACHER

I SOUGHT out, therefore, this same venerable man, whose fame, in truth, was more the result of long-established custom than of the potency of his own talent or intellect. If any one came to him impelled by doubt on any subject, he went away more doubtful still. He was wonderful, indeed, in the eyes of these who only listened to him, but those who asked him questions perforce held him as nought. He had a miraculous flow of words, but they were contemptible in meaning and quite void of reason. When he kindled a fire, he filled his house with smoke and illumined it not at all. He was a tree which seemed noble to those who gazed upon its leaves from afar, but to those who came nearer and examined it more closely was revealed its barrenness. When, therefore, I had come to this tree that I might pluck the fruit thereof, I discovered that it was indeed the fig tree which Our Lord cursed (Matthew xxi, 19; Mark xi, 13), or that ancient oak to which Lucan likened Pompey, saying:

> ". . . he stands, the shade of a name once
>   mighty,
> Like to the towering oak in the midst of the
>   fruitful field."
>   (Lucan, "Pharsalia," IV, 135.)

It was not long before I made this discovery, and

[10]

Theologian — studies sacred scripture

stretched myself lazily in the shade of that same tree. I went to his lectures less and less often, a thing which some among his eminent followers took sorely to heart, because they interpreted it as a mark of contempt for so illustrious a teacher. Thenceforth they secretly sought to influence him against me, and by their vile insinuations made me hated of him. It chanced, moreover, that one day, after the exposition of certain texts, we scholars were jesting among ourselves, and one of them, seeking to draw me out, asked me what I thought of the lectures on the Books of Scripture. I, who had as yet studied only the sciences, replied that following such lectures seemed to me most useful in so far as the salvation of the soul was concerned, but that it appeared quite extraordinary to me that educated persons should not be able to understand the sacred books simply by studying them themselves, together with the glosses thereon, and without the aid of any teacher. Most of those who were present mocked at me, and asked whether I myself could do as I had said, or whether I would dare to undertake it. I answered that if they wished, I was ready to try it. Forthwith they cried out and jeered all the more. "Well and good," said they; "we agree to the test. Pick out and give us an exposition of some doubtful passage in the Scriptures, so that we can put this boast of yours to the proof." And they all chose that most obscure prophecy of Ezekiel.

I accepted the challenge, and invited them to attend

Says you do not need a teacher to use a scripture

a lecture on the very next day. Whereupon they under-took to give me good advice, saying that I should by no means make undue haste in so important a matter, but that I ought to devote a much longer space to working out my exposition and offsetting my inexperience by diligent toil. To this I replied indignantly that it was my wont to win success, not by routine, but by ability. I added that I would abandon the test altogether unless they would agree not to put off their attendance at my lecture. In truth at this first lecture of mine only a few were present, for it seemed quite absurd to all of them that I, hitherto so inexperienced in discussing the Scriptures, should attempt the thing so hastily. However, this lecture gave such satisfaction to all those who heard it that they spread its praises abroad with notable enthusiasm, and thus compelled me to continue my interpretation of the sacred text. When word of this was bruited about, those who had stayed away from the first lecture came eagerly, some to the second and more to the third, and all of them were eager to write down the glosses which I had begun on the first day, so as to have them from the very beginning.

Says he is the best commentator on scriptures around

CHAPTER IV

OF THE PERSECUTION HE HAD FROM HIS TEACHER ANSELM

Now this venerable man of whom I have spoken was acutely smitten with envy, and straightway incited, as I have already mentioned, by the insinuations of sundry persons, began to persecute me for my lecturing on the Scriptures no less bitterly than my former master, William, had done for my work in philosophy. At that time there were in this old man's school two who were considered far to excel all the others: Alberic of Rheims and Lotulphe the Lombard. The better opinion these two held of themselves, the more they were incensed against me. Chiefly at their suggestion, as it afterwards transpired, yonder venerable coward had the impudence to forbid me to carry on any further in his school the work of preparing glosses which I had thus begun. The pretext he alleged was that if by chance in the course of this work I should write anything containing blunders—as was likely enough in view of my lack of training—the thing might be imputed to him. When this came to the ears of his scholars, they were filled with indignation at so undisguised a manifestation of spite, the like of which had never been directed against any one before. The more obvious this rancour became, the more it redounded to my honour, and his persecution did nought save to make me more famous.

[13]

CHAPTER V

OF HOW HE RETURNED TO PARIS AND FINISHED THE GLOSSES WHICH HE HAD BEGUN AT LAON

AND SO, after a few days, I returned to Paris, and there for several years I peacefully directed the school which formerly had been destined for me, nay, even offered to me, but from which I had been driven out. At the very outset of my work there, I set about completing the glosses on Ezekiel which I had begun at Laon. These proved so satisfactory to all who read them that they came to believe me no less adept in lecturing on theology than I had proved myself to be in the field of philosophy. Thus my school was notably increased in size by reason of my lectures on subjects of both these kinds, and the amount of financial profit as well as glory which it brought me cannot be concealed from you, for the matter was widely talked of. But prosperity always puffs up the foolish, and worldly comfort enervates the soul, rendering it an easy prey to carnal temptations. Thus I, who by this time had come to regard myself as the only philosopher remaining in the whole world, and had ceased to fear any further disturbance of my peace, began to loosen the rein on my desires, although hitherto I had always lived in the utmost continence. And the greater progress I made in my lecturing on philosophy or theology, the more I departed alike from the practice of the philosophers and the spirit of the divines in the uncleanness of

[14]

went to Laon to lecorn sacred scriphres

my life. For it is well known, methinks, that philosophers, and still more those who have devoted their lives to arousing the love of sacred study, have been strong above all else in the beauty of chastity.

Thus did it come to pass that while I was utterly absorbed in pride and sensuality, divine grace, the cure for both diseases, was forced upon me, even though I, forsooth, would fain have shunned it. First was I punished for my sensuality, and then for my pride. For my sensuality I lost those things whereby I practiced it; for my pride, engendered in me by my knowledge of letters— and it is even as the Apostle said: "Knowledge puffeth itself up" (I Cor. viii, 1)— I knew the humiliation of seeing burned the very book in which I most gloried. And now it is my desire that you should know the stories of these two happenings, understanding them more truly from learning the very facts than from hearing what is spoken of them, and in the order in which they came about. Because I had ever held in abhorrence the foulness of prostitutes, because I had diligently kept myself from all excesses and from association with the women of noble birth who attended the school, because I knew so little of the common talk of ordinary people, perverse and subtly flattering chance gave birth to an occasion for casting me lightly down from the heights of my own exaltation. Nay, in such case not even divine goodness could redeem one who, having been so proud, was brought to such shame, were it not for the blessed gift of grace.

CHAPTER VI

OF HOW, BROUGHT LOW BY HIS LOVE FOR HÉLOÏSE, HE WAS WOUNDED IN BODY AND SOUL

Now there dwelt in that same city of Paris a certain young girl named Héloïse, the niece of a canon who was called Fulbert. Her uncle's love for her was equalled only by his desire that she should have the best education which he could possibly procure for her. Of no mean beauty, she stood out above all by reason of her abundant knowledge of letters. Now this virtue is rare among women, and for that very reason it doubly graced the maiden, and made her the most worthy of renown in the entire kingdom. It was this young girl whom I, after carefully considering all those qualities which are wont to attract lovers, determined to unite with myself in the bonds of love, and indeed the thing seemed to me very easy to be done. So distinguished was my name, and I possessed such advantages of youth and comeliness, that no matter what woman I might favour with my love, I dreaded rejection of none. Then, too, I believed that I could win the maiden's consent all the more easily by reason of her knowledge of letters and her zeal therefor; so, even if we were parted, we might yet be together in thought with the aid of written messages. Perchance, too, we might be able to write more boldly than we could speak, and thus at all times could we live in joyous intimacy.

[16]

very confident person

Thus, utterly aflame with my passion for this maiden, I sought to discover means whereby I might have daily and familiar speech with her, thereby the more easily to win her consent. For this purpose I persuaded the girl's uncle, with the aid of some of his friends, to take me into his household—for he dwelt hard by my school—in return for the payment of a small sum. My pretext for this was that the care of my own household was a serious handicap to my studies, and likewise burdened me with an expense far greater than I could afford. Now, he was a man keen in avarice, and likewise he was most desirous for his niece that her study of letters should ever go forward, so, for these two reasons, I easily won his consent to the fulfillment of my wish, for he was fairly agape for my money, and at the same time believed that his niece would vastly benefit by my teaching. More even than this, by his own earnest entreaties he fell in with my desires beyond anything I had dared to hope, opening the way for my love; for he entrusted her wholly to my guidance, begging me to give her instruction whensoever I might be free from the duties of my school, no matter whether by day or by night, and to punish her sternly if ever I should find her negligent of her tasks. In all this the man's simplicity was nothing short of astounding to me; I should not have been more smitten with wonder if he had entrusted a tender lamb to the care of a ravenous wolf. When he had thus given her into my charge, not alone to be taught but even to be disciplined, what had he done save to give free scope to my desires, and to offer me every opportunity, even if I had not sought it, to bend her to my will with threats and blows if I failed to do so with caresses? There were, however, two things which particularly served to allay any foul suspicion: his own love for his niece, and my former reputation for continence.

Why should I say more? We were united first in the dwelling that sheltered our love, and then in the hearts that burned with it. Under the pretext of study we spent our hours in the happiness of love, and learning held out to us the secret opportunities that our passion craved. Our speech was more of love than of the books which lay open before us; our kisses far outnumbered our reasoned words. Our hands sought less the book than each other's bosoms; love drew our eyes together far more than the lesson drew them to the pages of our text. In order that there might be no suspicion, there were, indeed, sometimes blows, but love gave them, not anger; they were the marks, not of wrath, but of a tenderness surpassing the most fragrant balm in sweetness. What followed? No degree in love's progress was left untried by our passion, and if love itself could imagine any wonder as yet unknown, we discovered it. And our inexperience of such delights made us all the more ardent in our pursuit of them, so that our thirst for one another was still unquenched.

In measure as this passionate rapture absorbed me

more and more, I devoted ever less time to philosophy and to the work of the school. Indeed it became loathsome to me to go to the school or to linger there; the labour, moreover, was very burdensome, since my nights were vigils of love and my days of study. My lecturing became utterly careless and lukewarm; I did nothing because of inspiration, but everything merely as a matter of habit. I had become nothing more than a reciter of my former discoveries, and though I still wrote poems, they dealt with love, not with the secrets of philosophy. Of these songs you yourself well know how some have become widely known and have been sung in many lands, chiefly, methinks, by those who delighted in the things of this world. As for the sorrow, the groans, the lamentations of my students when they perceived the preoccupation, nay, rather the chaos, of my mind, it is hard even to imagine them.

A thing so manifest could deceive only a few, no one, methinks, save him whose shame it chiefly bespoke, the girl's uncle, Fulbert. The truth was often enough hinted to him, and by many persons, but he could not believe it, partly, as I have said, by reason of his boundless love for his niece, and partly because of the well-known continence of my previous life. Indeed we do not easily suspect shame in those whom we most cherish, nor can there be the blot of foul suspicion on devoted love. Of this St. Jerome in his epistle to Sabinianus (Epist. 48) says: "We are wont to be the last to know the evils of our own

Since he fell in love, his lectures had no substance any more households, and to be ignorant of the sins of our children and our wives, though our neighbours sing them aloud." But no matter how slow a matter may be in disclosing itself, it is sure to come forth at last, nor is it easy to hide from one what is known to all. So, after the lapse of several months, did it happen with us. Oh, how great was the uncle's grief when he learned the truth, and how bitter was the sorrow of the lovers when we were forced to part! With what shame was I overwhelmed, with what contrition smitten because of the blow which had fallen on her I loved, and what a tempest of misery burst over her by reason of my disgrace! Each grieved most, not for himself, but for the other. Each sought to allay, not his own sufferings, but those of the one he loved. The very sundering of our bodies served but to link our souls closer together; the plentitude of the love which was denied to us inflamed us more than ever. Once the first wildness of shame had passed, it left us more shameless than before, and as shame died within us the cause of it seemed to us ever more desirable. And so it chanced with us as, in the stories that the poets tell, it once happened with Mars and Venus when they were caught together.

It was not long after this that Héloïse found that she was pregnant, and of this she wrote to me in the utmost exultation, at the same time asking me to consider what had best be done. Accordingly, on a night when her uncle was absent, we carried out the plan we had determined on, and I stole her secretly away from her uncle's house, sending her without delay to my own country. She remained there with my sister until she gave birth to a son, whom she named Astrolabe. Meanwhile her uncle, after his return, was almost mad with grief; only one who had then seen him could rightly guess the burning agony of his sorrow and the bitterness of his shame. What steps to take against me, or what snares to set for me, he did not know. If he should kill me or do me some bodily hurt, he feared greatly lest his dear-loved niece should be made to suffer for it among my kinsfolk. He had no power to seize me and imprison me somewhere against my will, though I make no doubt he would have done so quickly enough had he been able or dared, for I had taken measures to guard against any such attempt.

At length, however, in pity for his boundless grief, and bitterly blaming myself for the suffering which my love had brought upon him through the baseness of the deception I had practiced, I went to him to entreat his forgiveness, promising to make any amends that he himself might decree. I pointed out that what had happened could not seem incredible to any one who had ever felt the power of love, or who remembered how, from the very beginning of the human race, women had cast down even the noblest men to utter ruin. And in order to make amends even beyond his extremest hope, I offered to marry her whom I had seduced, provided only the thing could be kept secret, so that I might suffer no loss of reputation thereby. To this he gladly assented, pledging his own faith and that of his kindred, and sealing with kisses the pact which I had sought of him—and all this that he might the more easily betray me.

CHAPTER VII

OF THE ARGUMENTS OF HÉLOÏSE AGAINST WEDLOCK— OF HOW NONE THE LESS HE MADE HER HIS WIFE

ORTHWITH I repaired to my own country, and brought back thence my mistress, that I might make her my wife. She, however, most violently disapproved of this, and for two chief reasons: the danger thereof, and the disgrace which it would bring upon me. She swore that her uncle would never be appeased by such satisfaction as this, as, indeed, afterwards proved only too true. She asked how she could ever glory in me if she should make me thus inglorious, and should shame herself along with me. What penalties, she said, would the world rightly demand of her if she should rob it of so shining a light! What curses would follow such a loss to the Church, what tears among the philosophers would result from such a marriage! How unfitting, how lamentable it would be for me, whom nature had made for the whole world, to devote myself to one woman solely, and to subject myself to such humiliation! She vehemently rejected this marriage, which she felt would be in every way ignominious and burdensome to me.

Besides dwelling thus on the disgrace to me, she reminded me of the hardships of married life, to the avoidance of which the Apostle exhorts us, saying: "Art thou loosed from a wife? seek not a wife. But and if thou marry, thou hast not sinned; and if a virgin marry, she hath not sinned. Nevertheless such shall have trouble in the flesh: but I spare you" (1 Cor. vii, 27). And again: "But I would have you to be free from cares" (1 Cor. vii, 32). But if I would heed neither the counsel of the Apostle nor the exhortations of the saints regarding this heavy yoke of matrimony, she bade me at least consider the advice of the philosophers, and weigh carefully what had been written on this subject either by them or concerning their lives. Even the saints themselves have often and earnestly spoken on this subject for the purpose of warning us. Thus St. Jerome, in his first book against Jovinianus, makes Theophrastus set forth in great detail the intolerable annoyances and the endless disturbances of married life, demonstrating with the most convincing arguments that no wise man should ever have a wife, and concluding his reasons for this philosophic exhortation with these words: "Who among Christians would not be overwhelmed by such arguments as these advanced by Theophrastus?"

Again, in the same work, St. Jerome tells how Cicero, asked by Hircius after his divorce of Terentia whether he would marry the sister of Hircius, replied that he would do no such thing, saying that he could not devote himself to a wife and to philosophy at the same time. Cicero does not, indeed, precisely speak of "devoting himself," but he does add that he did not wish to undertake anything which might rival his study of philosophy in its demands upon him.

Then, turning from the consideration of such hindrances to the study of philosophy, Héloïse bade me observe what were the conditions of honourable wedlock. What possible concord could there be between scholars and domestics, between authors and cradles, between books or tablets and distaffs, between the stylus or the pen and the spindle? What man, intent on his religious or philosophical meditations, can possibly endure the whining of children, the lullabies of the nurse seeking to quiet them, or the noisy confusion of family life? Who can endure the continual untidiness of children? The rich, you may reply, can do this, because they have palaces or houses containing many rooms, and because their wealth takes no thought of expense and protects them from daily worries. But to this the answer is that the condition of philosophers is by no means that of the wealthy, nor can those whose minds are occupied with riches and worldly cares find time for religious or philosophical study. For this reason the renowned philosophers of old utterly despised the world, fleeing from its perils rather than reluctantly giving them up, and denied themselves all its delights in order that they might repose in the embraces of philosophy alone. One of them, and the greatest of all, Seneca, in his advice to Lucilius, says: "Philosophy is not a thing to be studied only in hours of leisure; we must give up everything else to devote ourselves to it, for no amount of time is really sufficient thereto" (Epist. 73).

It matters little, she pointed out, whether one abandons the study of philosophy completely or merely interrupts it, for it can never remain at the point where it was thus interrupted. All other occupations must be resisted; it is vain to seek to adjust life to include them, and they must simply be eliminated. This view is maintained, for example, in the love of God by those among us who are truly called monastics, and in the love of wisdom by all those who have stood out among men as sincere philosophers. For in every race, gentiles or Jews or Christians, there have always been a few who excelled their fellows in faith or in the purity of their lives, and who were set apart from the multitude by their continence or by their abstinence from worldly pleasures.

Among the Jews of old there were the Nazarites, who consecrated themselves to the Lord, some of them the sons of the prophet Elias and others the followers of Eliseus, the monks of whom, on the authority of St. Jerome (Epist. 4 and 13), we read in the Old Testament. More recently there were the three philosophical sects which Josephus defines in his Book of Antiquities (xviii, 2), calling them the Pharisees, the Sadducees and the Essenes. In our times, furthermore, there are the monks who imitate either the communal life of the Apostles or the earlier and solitary life of John. Among the gentiles there are, as has been said, the philosophers. Did they not apply the name of wisdom or philosophy as much to the religion of life as to the pursuit of learning, as we find from the origin of the word itself, and likewise from the testimony of the saints?

There is a passage on this subject in the eighth book of St. Augustine's "City of God," wherein he distinguishes between the various schools of philosophy. "The Italian school," he says, "had as its founder Pythagoras of Samos, who, it is said, originated the very word 'philosophy.' Before his time those who were regarded as conspicuous for the praiseworthiness of their lives were called wise men, but he, on being asked of his profession, replied that he was a philosopher, that is to say a student or a lover of wisdom, because it seemed to him unduly boastful to call himself a wise man." In this passage, therefore, when the phrase "conspicuous for the praiseworthiness of their lives" is used, it is evident that the wise, in other words the philosophers, were so called less because of their erudition than by reason of their virtuous lives. In what sobriety and continence these men lived it is not for me to prove by illustration, lest I should seem to instruct Minerva herself.

Now, she added, if laymen and gentiles, bound by no profession of religion, lived after this fashion, what ought you, a cleric and a canon, to do in order not to prefer base voluptuousness to your sacred duties, to prevent this Charybdis from sucking you down headlong, and to save yourself from being plunged shamelessly and irrevocably into such filth as this? If you care nothing for your privileges as a cleric, at least uphold your dignity as a philosopher. If you scorn the reverence due to God, let regard for your reputation temper your shamelessness. Remember that Socrates was chained to a wife, and by what a filthy accident he himself paid for this blot on philosophy, in order that others thereafter might be made more cautious by his example. Jerome thus mentions this affair, writing about Socrates in his first book against Jovinianus: "Once when he was withstanding a storm of reproaches which Xantippe was hurling at him from an upper story, he was suddenly drenched with foul slops; wiping his head, he said only, 'I knew there would be a shower after all that thunder.'"

Her final argument was that it would be dangerous for me to take her back to Paris, and that it would be far sweeter for her to be called my mistress than to be known as my wife; nay, too, that this would be more honourable for me as well. In such case, she said, love alone would hold me to her, and the strength of the marriage chain would not constrain us. Even if we should by chance be parted from time to time, the joy of our meetings would be all the sweeter by reason of its rarity. But when she found that she could not convince me or dissuade me from my folly by these and like arguments, and because she could not bear to offend me, with grievous sighs and tears she made an end of her resistance, saying: "Then there is no more left but this, that in our doom the sorrow yet to come shall be no less than the love we two have already known." Nor in this, as now the

Socrates is a good example why a philosopy
Should not be married

whole world knows, did she lack the spirit of prophecy.

So, after our little son was born, we left him in my sister's care, and secretly returned to Paris. A few days later, in the early morning, having kept our nocturnal vigil of prayer unknown to all in a certain church, we were united there in the benediction of wedlock, her uncle and a few friends of his and mine being present. We departed forthwith stealthily and by separate ways, nor thereafter did we see each other save rarely and in private, thus striving our utmost to conceal what we had done. But her uncle and those of his household, seeking solace for their disgrace, began to divulge the story of our marriage, and thereby to violate the pledge they had given me on this point. Héloïse, on the contrary, denounced her own kin and swore that they were speaking the most absolute lies. Her uncle, aroused to fury thereby, visited her repeatedly with punishments. No sooner had I learned this than I sent her to a convent of nuns at Argenteuil, not far from Paris, where she herself had been brought up and educated as a young girl. I had them make ready for her all the garments of a nun, suitable for the life of a convent, excepting only the veil, and these I bade her put on.

When her uncle and his kinsmen heard of this, they were convinced that now I had completely played them false and had rid myself forever of Héloïse by forcing her to become a nun. Violently incensed, they laid a plot against me, and one night, while I, all unsuspecting, was asleep in a secret room in my lodgings, they broke in with the help of one of my servants, whom they had bribed. There they had vengeance on me with a most cruel and most shameful punishment, such as astounded the whole world, for they cut off those parts of my body with which I had done that which was the cause of their sorrow. This done, straightway they fled, but two of them were captured, and suffered the loss of their eyes and their genital organs. One of these two was the aforesaid servant, who, even while he was still in my service, had been led by his avarice to betray me.

CHAPTER VIII

Of the Suffering of His Body—Of How He Became a Monk in the Monastery of St. Denis and Héloïse a Nun at Argenteuil

WHEN morning came the whole city was assembled before my dwelling. It is difficult, nay, impossible, for words of mine to describe the amazement which bewildered them, the lamentations they uttered, the uproar with which they harassed me, or the grief with which they increased my own suffering. Chiefly the clerics, and above all my scholars, tortured me with their intolerable lamentations and outcries, so that I suffered more intensely from their compassion than from the pain of my wound. In truth I felt the disgrace more than the hurt to my body, and was more afflicted with shame than with pain. My incessant thought was of the renown in which I had so much delighted, now brought low, nay, utterly blotted out, so swiftly by an evil chance. I saw, too, how justly God had punished me in that very part of my body whereby I had sinned. I perceived that there was indeed justice in my betrayal by him whom I had myself already betrayed; and then I thought how eagerly my rivals would seize upon this manifestation of justice, how this disgrace would bring bitter and enduring grief to my kindred and my friends, and how the tale of this amazing outrage would spread to the very ends of the earth.

What path lay open to me thereafter? How could I ever again hold up my head among men, when every finger should be pointed at me in scorn, every tongue speak my blistering shame, and when I should be a monstrous spectacle to all eyes? I was overwhelmed by the remembrance that, according to the dread letter of the law, God holds eunuchs in such abomination that men thus maimed are forbidden to enter a church, even as the unclean and filthy; nay, even beasts in such plight were not acceptable as sacrifices. Thus in Leviticus (xxii, 24) is it said: "Ye shall not offer unto the Lord that which hath its stones bruised, or crushed, or broken, or cut." And in Deuteronomy (xxiii, 1), "He that is wounded in the stones, or hath his privy member cut off, shall not enter into the congregation of the Lord."

I must confess that in my misery it was the overwhelming sense of my disgrace rather than any ardour for conversion to the religious life that drove me to seek the seclusion of the monastic cloister. Héloïse had already, at my bidding, taken the veil and entered a convent. Thus it was that we both put on the sacred garb, I in the abbey of St. Denis, and she in the convent of Argenteuil, of which I have already spoken. She, I remember well, when her fond friends sought vainly to deter her from submitting her fresh youth to the heavy and almost intolerable yoke of monastic life, sobbing and weeping replied in the words of Cornelia:

". . . O husband most noble,
Who ne'er shouldst have shared my couch! Has
	fortune such power
To smite so lofty a head? Why then was I wedded
Only to bring thee to woe? Receive now my sorrow,
The price I so gladly pay."

(Lucan, "Pharsalia," viii, 94.)

With these words on her lips did she go forthwith to
the altar, and lifted therefrom the veil, which had been
blessed by the bishop, and before them all she took the
vows of the religious life. For my part, scarcely had I re-
covered from my wound when clerics sought me in great
numbers, endlessly beseeching both my abbot and me
myself that now, since I was done with learning for the
sake of gain or renown, I should turn to it for the sole
love of God. They bade me care diligently for the talent
which God had committed to my keeping (Matthew,
xxv, 15), since surely He would demand it back from me
with interest. It was their plea that, inasmuch as of old
I had laboured chiefly in behalf of the rich, I should now
devote myself to the teaching of the poor. Therein above
all should I perceive how it was the hand of God that
had touched me, when I should devote my life to the
study of letters in freedom from the snares of the flesh
and withdrawn from the tumultuous life of this world.
Thus, in truth, should I become a philosopher less of this
world than of God.

The abbey, however, to which I had betaken myself

was utterly worldly and in its life quite scandalous. The abbot himself was as far below his fellows in his way of living and in the foulness of his reputation as he was above them in priestly rank. This intolerable state of things I often and vehemently denounced, sometimes in private talk and sometimes publicly, but the only result was that I made myself detested of them all. They gladly laid hold of the daily eagerness of my students to hear me as an excuse whereby they might be rid of me; and finally, at the insistent urging of the students themselves, and with the hearty consent of the abbot and the rest of the brotherhood, I departed thence to a certain hut, there to teach in my wonted way. To this place such a throng of students flocked that the neighbourhood could not afford shelter for them, nor the earth sufficient sustenance.

Here, as befitted my profession, I devoted myself chiefly to lectures on theology, but I did not wholly abandon the teaching of the secular arts, to which I was more accustomed, and which was particularly demanded of me. I used the latter, however, as a hook, luring my students by the bait of learning to the study of the true philosophy, even as the Ecclesiastical History tells of Origen, the greatest of all Christian philosophers. Since apparently the Lord had gifted me with no less persuasiveness in expounding the Scriptures than in lecturing on secular subjects, the number of my students in these two courses began to increase greatly, and the attendance at all the other schools was correspondingly diminished. Thus I aroused the envy and hatred of the other teachers. Those who sought to belittle me in every possible way took advantage of my absence to bring two principal charges against me: first, that it was contrary to the monastic profession to be concerned with the study of secular books; and, second, that I had presumed to teach theology without ever having been taught therein myself. This they did in order that my teaching of every kind might be prohibited, and to this end they continually stirred up bishops, archbishops, abbots and whatever other dignitaries of the Church they could reach.

CHAPTER IX

OF HIS BOOK ON THEOLOGY AND HIS PERSECUTION AT THE HANDS OF HIS FELLOW STUDENTS— OF THE COUNCIL AGAINST HIM

IT so happened that at the outset I devoted myself to analysing the basis of our faith through illustrations based on human understanding, and I wrote for my students a certain tract on the unity and trinity of God. This I did because they were always seeking for rational and philosophical explanations, asking rather for reasons they could understand than for mere words, saying that it was futile to utter words which the intellect could not possibly follow, that nothing could be believed unless it could first be understood, and that it was absurd for any one to preach to others a thing which neither he himself nor those whom he sought to teach could comprehend. Our Lord Himself maintained this same thing when He said: "They are blind leaders of the blind" (Matthew, xv, 14).

Now, a great many people saw and read this tract, and it became exceedingly popular, its clearness appealing particularly to all who sought information on this subject. And since the questions involved are generally considered the most difficult of all, their complexity is taken as the measure of the subtlety of him who succeeds in answering them. As a result, my rivals became furiously angry, and summoned a council to take action against me, the chief instigators therein being my two intriguing enemies of former days, Alberic and Lotulphe. These two, now that both William and Anselm, our erstwhile teachers, were dead, were greedy to reign in their stead, and, so to speak, to succeed them as heirs. While they were directing the school at Rheims, they managed by repeated hints to stir up their archbishop, Rodolphe, against me, for the purpose of holding a meeting, or rather an ecclesiastical council, at Soissons, provided they could secure the approval of Conon, Bishop of Praeneste, at that time papal legate in France. Their plan was to summon me to be present at this council, bringing with me the famous book I had written regarding the Trinity. In all this, indeed, they were successful, and the thing happened according to their wishes.

Before I reached Soissons, however, these two rivals of mine so foully slandered me with both the clergy and the public that on the day of my arrival the people came near to stoning me and the few students of mine who had accompanied me thither. The cause of their anger was that they had been led to believe that I had preached and written to prove the existence of three gods. No sooner had I reached the city, therefore, than I went forthwith to the legate; to him I submitted my book for examination and judgment, declaring that if I had written anything repugnant to the Catholic faith, I was quite ready to correct it or otherwise to make satisfactory amends. The legate directed me to refer my book to the archbishop and to those same two rivals of mine, to the end that my accusers might also be my judges. So in my case was fulfilled the saying: "Even our enemies are our judges" (Deut. xxxii, 31).

These three, then, took my book and pawed it over and examined it minutely, but could find nothing therein which they dared to use as the basis for a public accusation against me. Accordingly they put off the condemnation of the book until the close of the council, despite their eagerness to bring it about. For my part, every day before the council convened I publicly discussed the Catholic faith in the light of what I had written, and all who heard me were enthusiastic in their approval alike of the frankness and the logic of my words. When the public and the clergy had thus learned something of the real character of my teaching, they began to say to one another: "Behold, now he speaks openly, and no one brings any charge against him. And this council, summoned, as we have heard, chiefly to take action upon his case, is drawing toward its end. Did the judges realize that the error might be theirs rather than his?"

As a result of all this, my rivals grew more angry day by day. On one occasion Alberic, accompanied by some of his students, came to me for the purpose of intimidating me, and, after a few bland words, said that he was amazed at something he had found in my book, to the effect that, although God had begotten God, I denied that God had begotten Himself, since there was only one God. I answered unhesitatingly: "I can give you an explanation of this if you wish it." "Nay," he replied, "I care nothing for human explanation or reasoning in such matters, but only for the words of authority." "Very well," I said; "turn the pages of my book and you will find the authority likewise." The book was at hand, for he had brought it with him. I turned to the passage I had in mind, which he had either not discovered or else passed over as containing nothing injurious to me. And it was God's will that I quickly found what I sought. This was the following sentence, under the heading "Augustine, On the Trinity, Book I": "Whosoever believes that it is within the power of God to beget Himself is sorely in error; this power is not in God, neither is it in any created thing, spiritual or corporeal. For there is nothing that can give birth to itself."

When those of his followers who were present heard this, they were amazed and much embarrassed. He himself, in order to keep his countenance, said: "Certainly, I understand all that." Then I added: "What I have to say further on this subject is by no means new, but apparently it has nothing to do with the case at issue, since you have asked for the word of authority only, and not for explanations. If, however, you care to consider logical explanations, I am prepared to demonstrate that, according to Augustine's statement, you have yourself fallen into a heresy in believing that a father can possibly be his own son." When Alberic heard this he was almost beside himself with rage, and straightway resorted to threats, asserting that neither my explanations nor my citations of authority would avail me aught in this case. With this he left me.

On the last day of the council, before the session convened, the legate and the archbishop deliberated with my rivals and sundry others as to what should be done about me and my book, this being the chief reason for their having come together. And since they had discovered nothing either in my speech or in what I had hitherto written which would give them a case against me, they were all reduced to silence, or at the most to maligning me in whispers. Then Geoffroi, Bishop of Chartres, who excelled the other bishops alike in the sincerity of his religion and in the importance of his see, spoke thus:

"You know, my lords, all who are gathered here, the doctrine of this man, what it is, and his ability, which has brought him many followers in every field to which he has devoted himself. You know how greatly he has lessened the renown of other teachers, both his masters and our own, and how he has spread as it were the offshoots of his vine from sea to sea. Now, if you impose a lightly considered judgment on him, as I cannot believe you will, you well know that even if mayhap you are in the right there are many who will be angered thereby, and that he will have no lack of defenders. Remember above all that we have found nothing in this book of his that lies before us whereon any open accusation can be based. Indeed it is true, as Jerome says: 'Fortitude openly displayed always creates rivals, and the lightning strikes the highest peaks.' Have a care, then, lest by violent action you only increase his fame, and lest we do more hurt to ourselves through envy than to him through justice. A false report, as that same wise man reminds us, is easily crushed, and a man's later life gives testimony as to his earlier deeds. If, then, you are disposed to take canonical action against him, his doctrine or his writings must be brought forward as evidence, and he must have free opportunity to answer his questioners. In that case, if he is found guilty or if he confesses his error, his lips can be wholly sealed. Consider the words of the blessed Nicodemus, who, desiring to free Our Lord Himself, said: 'Doth our law judge any man before it hear him and know what he doeth?'" (John, vii, 51).

When my rivals heard this they cried out in protest, saying: "This is wise counsel, forsooth, that we should strive against the wordiness of this man, whose arguments, or rather, sophistries, the whole world cannot resist!" And yet, methinks, it was far more difficult to strive against Christ Himself, for Whom, nevertheless, Nicodemus demanded a hearing in accordance with the dictates of the law. When the bishop could not win their assent to his proposals, he tried in another way to curb their hatred, saying that for the discussion of such an important case the few who were present were not enough, and that this matter required a more thorough examination. His further suggestion was that my abbot, who was there present, should take me back with him to our abbey, in other words to the monastery of St. Denis, and that there a large convocation of learned men should determine, on the basis of a careful investigation, what ought to be done. To this last proposal the legate consented, as did all the others.

Then the legate arose to celebrate mass before entering the council, and through the bishop sent me the permission which had been determined on, authorizing me to return to my monastery and there await such action as might be finally taken. But my rivals, perceiving that they would accomplish nothing if the trial were to be held outside of their own diocese, and in a place where they could have little influence on the verdict, and in truth having small wish that justice should be done, persuaded the archbishop that it would be a grave insult to him to transfer this case to another court, and that it would be dangerous for him if by chance I should thus be acquitted. They likewise went to the legate, and succeeded in so changing his opinion that finally they induced him to frame a new sentence, whereby he agreed to condemn my book without any further inquiry, to burn it forthwith in the sight of all, and to confine me for a year in another monastery. The argument they used was that it sufficed for the condemnation of my book that I had presumed to read it in public without the approval either of the Roman pontiff or of the Church, and that, furthermore, I had given it to many to be transcribed. Methinks it would be a notable blessing to the Christian faith if there were more who displayed a like presumption. The legate, however, being less skilled in law than he should have been, relied chiefly on the advice of the archbishop, and he, in turn, on that of my rivals. When the Bishop of Chartres got wind of this, he reported the whole conspiracy to me, and strongly urged me to endure meekly the manifest violence of their enmity. He bade me not to doubt that this violence would in the end react upon them and prove a blessing to me, and counseled me to have no fear of the confinement in a monastery, knowing that within a few days the legate himself, who was now acting under compulsion, would after his departure set me free. And thus he consoled me as best he might, mingling his tears with mine.

CHAPTER X

OF THE BURNING OF HIS BOOK—OF THE PERSECUTION
HE HAD AT THE HANDS OF HIS ABBOT
AND THE BRETHREN

STRAIGHTWAY upon my summons I went to the council, and there, without further examination or debate, did they compel me with my own hand to cast that memorable book of mine into the flames. Although my enemies appeared to have nothing to say while the book was burning, one of them muttered something about having seen it written therein that God the Father was alone omnipotent. This reached the ears of the legate, who replied in astonishment that he could not believe that even a child would make so absurd a blunder. "Our common faith," he said, "holds and sets forth that the Three are alike omnipotent." A certain Tirric, a schoolmaster, hearing this, sarcastically added the Athanasian phrase, "And yet there are not three omnipotent Persons, but only One."

This man's bishop forthwith began to censure him, bidding him desist from such treasonable talk, but he boldly stood his ground, and said, as if quoting the words of Daniel: " 'Are ye such fools, ye sons of Israel, that without examination or knowledge of the truth ye have condemned a daughter of Israel? Return again to the place of judgment,' (Daniel, xiii, 48—The History of Susanna) and there give judgment on the judge himself.

You have set up this judge, forsooth, for the instruction of faith and the correction of error, and yet, when he ought to give judgment, he condemns himself out of his own mouth. Set free today, with the help of God's mercy, one who is manifestly innocent, even as Susanna was freed of old from her false accusers."

Thereupon the archbishop arose and confirmed the legate's statement, but changed the wording thereof, as indeed was most fitting. "It is God's truth," he said, "that the Father is omnipotent, the Son is omnipotent, the Holy Spirit is omnipotent. And whosoever dissents from this is openly in error, and must not be listened to. Nevertheless, if it be your pleasure, it would be well that this our brother should publicly state before us all the faith that is in him, to the end that, according to its deserts, it may either be approved or else condemned and corrected."

When, however, I fain would have arisen to profess and set forth my faith, in order that I might express in my own words that which was in my heart, my enemies declared that it was not needful for me to do more than recite the Athanasian Symbol, a thing which any boy might do as well as I. And lest I should allege ignorance, pretending that I did not know the words by heart, they had a copy of it set before me to read. And read it I did as best I could for my groans and sighs and tears. Thereupon, as if I had been a convicted criminal, I was handed over to the Abbot of St. Médard, who was there present,

[45]

and led to his monastery as to a prison. And with this the council was immediately dissolved.

The abbot and the monks of the aforesaid monastery, thinking that I would remain long with them, received me with great exultation, and diligently sought to console me, but all in vain. O God, who dost judge justice itself, in what venom of the spirit, in what bitterness of mind, did I blame even Thee for my shame, accusing Thee in my madness! Full often did I repeat the lament of St. Anthony: "Kindly Jesus, where wert Thou?" The sorrow that tortured me, the shame that overwhelmed me, the desperation that wracked my mind, all these I could then feel, but even now I can find no words to express them. Comparing these new sufferings of my soul with those I had formerly endured in my body, it seemed that I was in very truth the most miserable among men. Indeed that earlier betrayal had become a little thing in comparison with this later evil, and I lamented the hurt to my fair name far more than the one to my body. The latter, indeed, I had brought upon myself through my own wrongdoing, but this other violence had come upon me solely by reason of the honesty of my purpose and my love of our faith, which had compelled me to write that which I believed.

The very cruelty and heartlessness of my punishment, however, made every one who heard the story vehement in censuring it, so that those who had a hand therein were soon eager to disclaim all responsibility, shouldering the blame on others. Nay, matters came to such a pass that even my rivals denied that they had had anything to do with the matter, and as for the legate, he publicly denounced the malice with which the French had acted. Swayed by repentance for his injustice, and feeling that he had yielded enough to satisfy their rancour, he shortly freed me from the monastery whither I had been taken, and sent me back to my own. Here, however, I found almost as many enemies as I had in the former days of which I have already spoken, for the vileness and shamelessness of their way of living made them realize that they would again have to endure my censure.

After a few months had passed, chance gave them an opportunity by which they sought to destroy me. It happened that one day, in the course of my reading, I came upon a certain passage of Bede, in his commentary on the Acts of the Apostles, wherein he asserts that Dionysius the Areopagite was the bishop, not of Athens, but of Corinth. Now, this was directly counter to the belief of the monks, who were wont to boast that their Dionysius, or Denis, was not only the Areopagite but was likewise proved by his acts to have been the Bishop of Athens. Having thus found this testimony of Bede's in contradiction of our own tradition, I showed it somewhat jestingly to sundry of the monks who chanced to be near. Wrathfully they declared that Bede was no better than a liar, and that they had a far more trustworthy authority in the person of Hilduin, a former abbot of theirs, who had travelled for a long time throughout Greece for the purpose of investigating this very question. He, they insisted, had by his writings removed all possible doubt on the subject, and had securely established the truth of the traditional belief.

One of the monks went so far as to ask me brazenly which of the two, Bede or Hilduin, I considered the better authority on this point. I replied that the authority of Bede, whose writings are held in high esteem by the whole Latin Church, appeared to me the better. Thereupon in a great rage they began to cry out that at last I had openly proved the hatred I had always felt for our monastery, and that I was seeking to disgrace it in the eyes of the whole kingdom, robbing it of the honour in which it had particularly gloried, by thus denying that the Areopagite was their patron saint. To this I answered that I had never denied the fact, and that I did not much care whether their patron was the Areopagite or some one else, provided only he had received his crown from God. Thereupon they ran to the abbot and told him of the misdemeanour with which they charged me.

The abbot listened to their story with delight, rejoicing at having found a chance to crush me, for the greater vileness of his life made him fear me more even than the rest did. Accordingly he summoned his council, and when the brethren had assembled he violently threatened me, declaring that he would straightway send me to the king, by him to be punished for having thus sullied his crown and the glory of his royalty. And until he should hand me over to the king, he ordered that I should be closely guarded. In vain did I offer to submit to the customary discipline if I had in any way been guilty. Then, horrified at their wickedness, which seemed to crown the ill fortune I had so long endured, and in utter despair at the apparent conspiracy of the whole world against me, I fled secretly from the monastery by night, helped thereto by some of the monks who took pity on me, and likewise aided by some of my scholars.

I made my way to a region where I had formerly dwelt, hard by the lands of Count Theobald (of Champagne). He himself had some slight acquaintance with me, and had compassion on me by reason of my persecutions, of which the story had reached him. I found a home there within the walls of Provins, in a priory of the monks of Troyes, the prior of which had in former days known me well and shown me much love. In his joy at my coming he cared for me with all diligence. It chanced, however, that one day my abbot came to Provins to see the count on certain matters of business. As soon as I had learned of this, I went to the count, the prior accompanying me, and besought him to intercede in my behalf with the abbot. I asked no more than that the abbot should absolve me of the charge against me, and give me permission to live the monastic life wheresoever I could find a suitable place. The abbot, however, and those who were with him took the matter under advisement, saying that they would give the count an answer the day before they departed. It appeared from their words that they thought I wished to go to some other abbey, a thing which they regarded as an immense disgrace to their own. They had, indeed, taken particular pride in the fact that, upon my conversion, I had come to them, as if scorning all other abbeys, and accordingly they considered that it would bring great shame upon them if I should now desert their abbey and seek another. For this reason they refused to listen either to my own plea or to that of the count. Furthermore, they threatened me with excommunication unless I should instantly return; likewise they forbade the prior with whom I had taken refuge to keep me longer, under pain of sharing my excommunication. When we heard this both the prior and I were stricken with fear. The abbot went away still obdurate, but a few days thereafter he died.

As soon as his successor had been named, I went to him, accompanied by the Bishop of Meaux, to try if I might win from him the permission I had vainly sought of his predecessor. At first he would not give his assent, but finally, through the intervention of certain friends of mine, I secured the right to appeal to the king and his council, and in this way I at last obtained what I sought. The royal seneschal, Stephen, having summoned the abbot and his subordinates that they might state their case, asked them why they wanted to keep me against my will. He pointed out that this might easily bring them into evil repute, and certainly could do them no good, seeing that their way of living was utterly incompatible with mine. I knew it to be the opinion of the royal council that the irregularities in the conduct of this abbey would tend to bring it more and more under the control of the king, making it increasingly useful and likewise profitable to him, and for this reason I had good hope of easily winning the support of the king and those about him.

Thus, indeed, did it come to pass. But in order that the monastery might not be shorn of any of the glory which it had enjoyed by reason of my sojourn there, they granted me permission to betake myself to any solitary place I might choose, provided only I did not put myself under the rule of any other abbey. This was agreed upon and confirmed on both sides in the presence of the king and his councellors. Forthwith I sought out a lonely spot known to me of old in the region of Troyes, and there, on a bit of land which had been given to me, and with the approval of the bishop of the district, I built with reeds and stalks my first oratory in the name of the Holy Trinity. And there concealed, with but one comrade, a certain cleric, I was able to sing over and over again to the Lord: "Lo, then would I wander far off, and remain in the wilderness" (Ps. IV, 7).

CHAPTER XI

OF HIS TEACHING IN THE WILDERNESS

No sooner had scholars learned of my retreat than they began to flock thither from all sides, leaving their towns and castles to dwell in the wilderness. In place of their spacious houses they built themselves huts; instead of dainty fare they lived on the herbs of the field and coarse bread; their soft beds they exchanged for heaps of straw and rushes, and their tables were piles of turf. In very truth you may well believe that they were like those philosophers of old of whom Jerome tells us in his second book against Jovinianus.

"Through the senses," says Jerome, "as through so many windows, do vices win entrance to the soul. The metropolis and citadel of the mind cannot be taken unless the army of the foe has first rushed in through the gates. If any one delights in the games of the circus, in the contests of athletes, in the versatility of actors, in the beauty of women, in the glitter of gems and raiment, or in aught else like to these, then the freedom of his soul is made captive through the windows of his eyes, and thus is fulfilled the prophecy: 'For death is come up into our windows' (Jer. ix, 21). And then, when the wedges of doubt have, as it were, been driven into the citadels of our minds through these gateways, where will be its liberty? where its fortitude? where its thought of God? Most of all does the sense of touch paint for itself the pictures of past raptures, compelling the soul to dwell fondly upon remembered iniquities, and so to practice in imagination those things which reality denies to it.

"Heeding such counsel, therefore, many among the philosophers forsook the thronging ways of the cities and the pleasant gardens of the countryside, with their well-watered fields, their shady trees, the song of birds, the mirror of the fountain, the murmur of the stream, the many charms for eye and ear, fearing lest their souls should grow soft amid luxury and abundance of riches, and lest their virtue should thereby be defiled. For it is perilous to turn your eyes often to those things whereby you may some day be made captive, or to attempt the possession of that which it would go hard with you to do without. Thus the Pythagoreans shunned all companionship of this kind, and were wont to dwell in solitary and desert places. Nay, Plato himself, although he was a rich man, let Diogenes trample on his couch with muddy feet, and in order that he might devote himself to philosophy established his academy in a place remote from the city, and not only uninhabited but unhealthy as well. This he did in order that the onslaughts of lust might be broken by the fear and constant presence of disease, and that his followers might find no pleasure save in the things they learned."

Such a life, likewise, the sons of the prophets who were the followers of Eliseus are reported to have led. Of these Jerome also tells us, writing thus to the monk Rusticus as if describing the monks of those ancient days: "The sons of the prophets, the monks of whom we read in the Old Testament, built for themselves huts by the waters of the Jordan, and forsaking the throngs and the cities, lived on pottage and the herbs of the field" (Epist. iv).

Even so did my followers build their huts above the waters of the Arduzon, so that they seemed hermits rather than scholars. And as their number grew ever greater, the hardships which they gladly endured for the sake of my teaching seemed to my rivals to reflect new glory on me, and to cast new shame on themselves. Nor was it strange that they, who had done their utmost to hurt me, should grieve to see how all things worked together for my good, even though I was now, in the words of Jerome, afar from cities and the market place, from controversies and the crowded ways of men. And so, as Quintilian says, did envy seek me out even in my hiding place. Secretly my rivals complained and lamented one to another, saying: "Behold now, the whole world runs after him, and our persecution of him has done nought save to increase his glory. We strove to extinguish his fame, and we have but given it new brightness. Lo, in the cities scholars have at hand everything they may need, and yet, spurning the pleasures of the town, they seek out the barrenness of the desert, and of their own free will they accept wretchedness."

The thing which at that time chiefly led me to undertake the direction of a school was my intolerable poverty, for I had not strength enough to dig, and shame kept me from begging. And so, resorting once more to the art with which I was so familiar, I was compelled to substitute the service of the tongue for the labour of my hands. The students willingly provided me with whatsoever I needed in the way of food and clothing, and likewise took charge of the cultivation of the fields and paid for the erection of buildings, in order that material cares might not keep me from my studies. Since my oratory was no longer large enough to hold even a small part of their number, they found it necessary to increase its size, and in so doing they greatly improved it, building it of stone and wood. Although this oratory had been founded in honour of the Holy Trinity, and afterwards dedicated thereto, I now named it the Paraclete, mindful of how I had come there a fugitive and in despair, and had breathed into my soul something of the miracle of divine consolation.

Many of those who heard of this were greatly astonished, and some violently assailed my action, declaring that it was not permissible to dedicate a church exclusively to the Holy Spirit rather than to God the Father. They held, according to an ancient tradition, that it must be dedicated either to the Son alone or else to the entire Trinity. The error which led them into this false accusation resulted from their failure to perceive the identity of the Paraclete with the Spirit Paraclete. Even as the whole Trinity, or any Person in the Trinity, may rightly be called God or Helper, so likewise may It be termed the Paraclete, that is to say the Consoler. These are the words of the Apostle: "Blessed be God, even the Father of our Lord Jesus Christ, the Father of mercies, and the God of all comfort; who comforteth us in all our tribulation" (2 Cor. i, 3). And likewise the word of truth says: "And he shall give you another comforter" (Greek "another Paraclete," John, xiv, 16).

Nay, since every church is consecrated equally in the name of the Father, the Son and the Holy Spirit, without any difference in their possession thereof, why should not the house of God be dedicated to the Father or to the Holy Spirit, even as it is to the Son? Who would presume to erase from above the door the name of him who is the master of the house? And since the Son offered Himself as a sacrifice to the Father, and accordingly in the ceremonies of the mass the prayers are offered particularly to the Father, and the immolation of the Host is made to Him, why should the altar not be held to be chiefly His to whom above all the supplication and sacrifice are made? Is it not called more rightly the altar of Him who receives than of Him who makes the sacrifice? Who would admit that an altar is that of the Holy Cross, or of the Sepulchre, or of St. Michael, or John, or Peter, or of any other saint, unless either he himself was sacrificed there or else special sacrifices and prayers are made there to him? Methinks the altars and temples of certain ones among these saints are not held to be idolatrous even though they are used for special sacrifices and prayers to their patrons.

Some, however, may perchance argue that churches are not built or altars dedicated to the Father because there is no feast which is solemnized especially for Him. But while this reasoning holds good as regards the Trinity itself, it does not apply in the case of the Holy Spirit. For this Spirit, from the day of Its advent, has had Its special feast of the Pentecost, even as the Son has had since His coming upon earth His feast of the Nativity. Even as the Son was sent into this world, so did the Holy Spirit descend upon the disciples, and thus does It claim Its special religious rites. Nay, it seems more fitting to dedicate a temple to It than to either of the other Persons of the Trinity, if we but carefully study the apostolic authority, and consider the workings of this Spirit Itself. To none of the three Persons did the apostle dedicate a special temple save to the Holy Spirit alone. He does not speak of a temple of the Father, or a temple of the Son, as he does of a temple of the Holy Spirit, writing thus in his first epistle to the Corinthians: "But he that is joined unto the Lord is one spirit." (I Cor. vi, 17). And again: "What? know ye not that your body is the temple of the Holy Spirit which is in you, which ye have of God, and ye are not your own?" (ib. 19).

Who is there who does not know that the sacraments of God's blessings pertaining to the Church are particularly ascribed to the operation of divine grace, by which is meant the Holy Spirit? Forsooth we are born again of water and of the Holy Spirit in baptism, and thus from the very beginning is the body made, as it were, a special temple of God. In the successive sacraments, moreover, the seven-fold grace of the Spirit is added, whereby this same temple of God is made beautiful and is consecrated. What wonder is it, then, if to that Person to Whom the apostle assigned a spiritual temple we should dedicate a material one? Or to what Person can a church be more rightly said to belong than to Him to Whom all the blessings which the church administers are particularly ascribed? It was not, however, with the thought of dedicating my oratory to one Person that I first called it the Paraclete, but for the reason I have already told, that in this spot I found consolation. None the less, even if I had done it for the reason attributed to me, the departure from the usual custom would have been in no way illogical.

CHAPTER XII

Of the Persecution Directed against Him by Sundry New Enemies or, as it Were, Apostles

And so I dwelt in this place, my body indeed hidden away, but my fame spreading throughout the whole world, till its echo reverberated mightily—echo, that fancy of the poet's, which has so great a voice, and nought beside. My former rivals, seeing that they themselves were now powerless to do me hurt, stirred up against me certain new apostles in whom the world put great faith. One of these (Norbert of Prémontré) took pride in his position as canon of a regular order; the other (Bernard of Clairvaux) made it his boast that he had revived the true monastic life. These two ran hither and yon preaching and shamelessly slandering me in every way they could, so that in time they succeeded in drawing down on my head the scorn of many among those having authority, among both the clergy and the laity. They spread abroad such sinister reports of my faith as well as of my life that they turned even my best friends against me, and those who still retained something of their former regard for me were fain to disguise it in every possible way by reason of their fear of these two men.

God is my witness that whensoever I learned of the convening of a new assemblage of the clergy, I believed that it was done for the express purpose of my condemnation. Stunned by this fear like one smitten with a thunderbolt, I daily expected to be dragged before their councils or assemblies as a heretic or one guilty of impiety. Though I seem to compare a flea with a lion, or an ant with an elephant, in very truth my rivals persecuted me no less bitterly than the heretics of old hounded St. Athanasius. Often, God knows, I sank so deep in despair that I was ready to leave the world of Christendom and go forth among the heathen, paying them a stipulated tribute in order that I might live quietly a Christian life among the enemies of Christ. It seemed to me that such people might indeed be kindly disposed toward me, particularly as they would doubtless suspect me of being no good Christian, imputing my flight to some crime I had committed, and would therefore believe that I might perhaps be won over to their form of worship.

CHAPTER XIII

OF THE ABBEY TO WHICH HE WAS CALLED AND OF
THE PERSECUTION HE HAD FROM HIS SONS,
THAT IS TO SAY THE MONKS, AND FROM THE
LORD OF THE LAND

WHILE I was thus afflicted with so great perturbation
of the spirit, and when the only way of escape seemed
to be for me to seek refuge with Christ among the enemies
of Christ, there came a chance whereby I thought I
could for a while avoid the plottings of my enemies. But
thereby I fell among Christians and monks who were far
more savage than heathens and more evil of life. The
thing came about in this wise. There was in lesser Brittany, in the bishopric of Vannes, a certain abbey of St.
Gildas at Ruits, then mourning the death of its shepherd.
To this abbey the elective choice of the brethren called
me, with the approval of the prince of that land, and I
easily secured permission to accept the post from my
own abbot and brethren. Thus did the hatred of the
French drive me westward, even as that of the Romans
drove Jerome toward the East. Never, God knows, would
I have agreed to this thing had it not been for my long-
ing for any possible means of escape from the sufferings
which I had borne so constantly.

The land was barbarous and its speech was unknown
to me; as for the monks, their vile and untameable way
of life was notorious almost everywhere. The people of

the region, too, were uncivilized and lawless. Thus, like one who in terror of the sword that threatens him dashes headlong over a precipice, and to shun one death for a moment rushes to another, I knowingly sought this new danger in order to escape from the former one. And there, amid the dreadful roar of the waves of the sea, where the land's end left me no further refuge in flight, often in my prayers did I repeat over and over again: "From the end of the earth will I cry unto Thee, when my heart is overwhelmed" (Ps. lxi, 2).

No one, methinks, could fail to understand how persistently that undisciplined body of monks, the direction of which I had thus undertaken, tortured my heart day and night, or how constantly I was compelled to think of the danger alike to my body and to my soul. I held it for certain that if I should try to force them to live according to the principles they had themselves professed, I should not survive. And yet, if I did not do this to the utmost of my ability, I saw that my damnation was assured. Moreover, a certain lord who was exceedingly powerful in that region had some time previously brought the abbey under his control, taking advantage of the state of disorder within the monastery to seize all the lands adjacent thereto for his own use, and he ground down the monks with taxes heavier than those which were extorted from the Jews themselves.

The monks pressed me to supply them with their daily necessities, but they held no property in common

Abalard dis approves of these things

which I might administer in their behalf, and each one, with such resources as he possessed, supported himself and his concubines, as well as his sons and daughters. They took delight in harassing me on this matter, and they stole and carried off whatsoever they could lay their hands on, to the end that my failure to maintain order might make me either give up trying to enforce discipline or else abandon my post altogether. Since the entire region was equally savage, lawless and disorganized, there was not a single man to whom I could turn for aid, for the habits of all alike were foreign to me. Outside the monastery the lord and his henchmen ceaselessly hounded me, and within its walls the brethren were forever plotting against me, so that it seemed as if the Apostle had had me and none other in mind when he said: "Without were fightings, within were fears" (II Cor. vii, 5).

I considered and lamented the uselessness and the wretchedness of my existence, how fruitless my life now was, both to myself and to others; how of old I had been of some service to the clerics whom I had now abandoned for the sake of these monks, so that I was no longer able to be of use to either; how incapable I had proved myself in everything I had undertaken or attempted, so that above all others I deserved the reproach, "This man began to build, and was not able to finish" (Luke xiv, 30). My despair grew still deeper when I compared the evils I had left behind with those to which I had come, for my former sufferings now seemed to me as nought. Full often did I groan: "Justly has this sorrow come upon me because I deserted the Paraclete, which is to say the Consoler, and thrust myself into sure desolation; seeking to shun threats I fled to certain peril."

The thing which tormented me most was the fact that, having abandoned my oratory, I could make no suitable provision for the celebration there of the divine office, for indeed the extreme poverty of the place would sarcely provide the necessities of one man. But the true Paraclete Himself brought me real consolation in the midst of this sorrow of mine, and made all due provision for His own oratory. For it chanced that in some manner or other, laying claim to it as having legally belonged in earlier days to his monastery, my abbot of St. Denis got possession of the abbey of Argenteuil, of which I have previously spoken, wherein she who was now my sister in Christ rather than my wife, Héloïse, had taken the veil. From this abbey he expelled by force all the nuns who had dwelt there, and of whom my former companion had become the prioress. The exiles being thus dispersed in various places, I perceived that this was an opportunity presented by God himself to me whereby I could make provision anew for my oratory. And so, returning thither, I bade her come to the oratory, together with some others from the same convent who had clung to her.

On their arrival there I made over to them the oratory, together with everything pertaining thereto, and subsequently, through the approval and assistance of the bishop of the district, Pope Innocent II promulgated a decree confirming my gift in perpetuity to them and their successors. And this refuge of divine mercy, which they served so devotedly, soon brought them consolation, even though at first their life there was one of want, and for a time of utter destitution. But the place proved itself a true Paraclete to them, making all those who dwelt round about feel pity and kindliness for the sisterhood. So that, methinks, they prospered more through gifts in a single year than I should have done if I had stayed there a hundred. True it is that the weakness of womankind makes their needs and sufferings appeal strongly to people's feelings, as likewise it makes their virtue all the more pleasing to God and man. And God granted such favour in the eyes of all to her who was now my sister, and who was in authority over the rest, that the bishops loved her as a daughter, the abbots as a sister, and the laity as a mother. All alike marvelled at her religious zeal, her good judgment and the sweetness of her incomparable patience in all things. The less often she allowed herself to be seen, shutting herself up in her cell to devote herself to sacred meditations and prayers, the more eagerly did those who dwelt without demand her presence and the spiritual guidance of her words.

CHAPTER XIV

OF THE EVIL REPORT OF HIS INIQUITY

BEFORE long all those who dwelt thereabouts began to censure me roundly, complaining that I paid far less attention to their needs than I might and should have done, and that at least I could do something for them through my preaching. As a result, I returned thither frequently, to be of service to them in whatsoever way I could. Regarding this there was no lack of hateful murmuring, and the thing which sincere charity induced me to do was seized upon by the wickedness of my detractors as the subject of shameless outcry. They declared that I, who of old could scarcely endure to be parted from her I loved, was still swayed by the delights of fleshly lust. Many times I thought of the complaint of St. Jerome in his letter to Asella regarding those women whom he was falsely accused of loving, when he said (Epist. xcix): "I am charged with nothing save the fact of my sex, and this charge is made only because Paula is setting forth to Jerusalem." And again: "Before I became intimate in the household of the saintly Paula, the whole city was loud in my praise, and nearly every one deemed me deserving of the highest honours of priesthood. But I know that my way to the kingdom of Heaven lies through good and evil report alike."

When I pondered over the injury which slander had done to so great a man as this, I was not a little consoled thereby. If my rivals, I told myself, could but find an equal cause for suspicion against me, with what accusations would they persecute me! But how is it possible for such suspicion to continue in my case, seeing that divine mercy has freed me therefrom by depriving me of all power to enact such baseness? How shameless is this latest accusation! In truth that which had happened to me so completely removes all suspicion of this iniquity among all men that those who wish to have their women kept under close guard employ eunuchs for that purpose, even as sacred history tells regarding Esther and the other damsels of King Ahasuerus (Esther ii, 5). We read, too, of that eunuch of great authority under Queen Candace who had charge of all her treasure, him to whose conversion and baptism the apostle Philip was directed by an angel (Acts viii, 27). Such men, in truth, are enabled to have far more importance and intimacy among modest and upright women by the fact that they are free from any suspicion of lust.

The sixth book of the Ecclesiastical History tells us that the greatest of all Christian philosophers, Origen, inflicted a like injury on himself with his own hand, in order that all suspicion of this nature might be completely done away with in his instruction of women in sacred doctrine. In this respect, I thought, God's mercy had been kinder to me than to him, for it was judged that he had acted most rashly and had exposed himself to no slight censure, whereas the thing had been done to me through the crime of another, thus preparing me for a task similar to his own. Moreover, it had been accomplished with much less pain, being so quick and sudden, for I was heavy with sleep when they laid hands on me, and felt scarcely any pain at all.

But alas, I thought, the less I then suffered from the wound, the greater is my punishment now through slander, and I am tormented far more by the loss of my reputation than I was by that of part of my body. For thus is it written: "A good name is rather to be chosen than great riches" (Prov. xxii, 1). And as St. Augustine tells us in a sermon of his on the life and conduct of the clergy, "He is cruel who, trusting in his conscience, neglects his reputation." Again he says: "Let us provide those things that are good, as the apostle bids us (Rom. xii, 17), not alone in the eyes of God, but likewise in the eyes of men. Within himself each one's conscience suffices, but for our own sakes our reputations ought not to be tarnished, but to flourish. Conscience and reputation are different matters: conscience is for yourself, reputation for your neighbour." Methinks the spite of such men as these my enemies would have accused the very Christ Himself, or those belonging to Him, prophets and apostles, or the other holy fathers, if such spite had existed in their time, seeing that they associated in such familiar intercourse with women, and this though they were whole of body. On this point St. Augustine, in his book on the duty of monks, proves that women followed our Lord Jesus Christ and the apostles as inseparable companions, even accompanying them when they preached (Chap. 4). "Faithful women," he says, "who were possessed of worldly wealth went with them, and ministered to them out of their wealth, so that they might lack none of those things which belong to the substance of life." And if any one does not believe that the apostles thus permitted saintly women to go about with them wheresoever they preached the Gospel, let him listen to the Gospel itself, and learn therefrom that in so doing they followed the example of the Lord. For in the Gospel it is written thus: "And it came to pass afterward, that He went throughout every city and village, preaching and showing the glad tidings of the kingdom of God: and the twelve were with Him, and certain women, which had been healed of evil spirits and infirmities, Mary called Magdalene, and Joanna the wife of Chuza, Herod's steward, and Susanna, and many others, which ministered unto Him of their substance" (Luke viii, 1-3).

Leo the Ninth, furthermore, in his reply to the letter of Parmenianus concerning monastic zeal, says: "We unequivocally declare that it is not permissible for a bishop, priest, deacon or subdeacon to cast off all responsibility for his own wife on the grounds of religious duty, so that he no longer provides her with food and clothing; albeit he may not have carnal intercourse with her. We read that thus did the holy apostles act, for St. Paul says: 'Have we not power to lead about a sister, a wife, as well as other apostles, and as the brethren of the Lord, and Cephas?' (I Cor. ix, 5). Observe, foolish man, that he does not say: 'have we not power to embrace a sister, a wife,' but he says 'to lead about,' meaning thereby that such women may lawfully be supported by them out of the wages of their preaching, but that there must be no carnal bond between them."

Certainly that Pharisee who spoke within himself of the Lord, saying: "This man, if He were a prophet, would have known who and what manner of woman this is that toucheth Him: for she is a sinner" (Luke vii, 39), might much more reasonably have suspected baseness of the Lord, considering the matter from a purely human standpoint, than my enemies could suspect it of me. One who had seen the mother of Our Lord entrusted to the care of the young man (John xix, 27), or who had beheld the prophets dwelling and sojourning with widows (I Kings xvii, 10), would likewise have had a far more logical ground for suspicion. And what would my calumniators have said if they had but seen Malchus, that captive monk of whom St. Jerome writes, living in the same hut with his wife? Doubtless they would have regarded it as criminal in the famous scholar to have highly commended what he thus saw, saying thereof: "There was a certain old man named Malchus, a native of this region, and his wife with him in his hut. Both of them were earnestly religious, and they so often passed the threshold of the church that you might have thought them the Zacharias and Elisabeth of the Gospel, saving only that John was not with them."

Why, finally, do such men refrain from slandering the holy fathers, of whom we frequently read, nay, and have even seen with our own eyes, founding convents for women and making provision for their maintenance, thereby following the example of the seven deacons whom the apostles sent before them to secure food and take care of the women? (Acts vi, 5). For the weaker sex needs the help of the stronger one to such an extent that the apostle proclaimed that the head of the woman is ever the man (I Cor. xi, 3), and in sign thereof he bade her ever wear her head covered (ib. 5). For this reason I marvel greatly at the customs which have crept into monasteries, whereby, even as abbots are placed in charge of the men, abbesses now are given authority over the women, and the women bind themselves in their vows to accept the same rules as the men. Yet in these rules there are many things which cannot possibly be carried out by women, either as superiors or in the lower orders. In many places we may even behold an inversion of the natural order of things, whereby the abbesses and nuns have authority over the clergy, and even over those who are themselves in charge of the people. The more power such women exercise over men, the more easily can they lead them into iniquitous desires, and in this way can lay a very heavy yoke upon their shoulders. It was with such things in mind that the satirist said:

"There is nothing more intolerable than a rich woman."

(Juvenal, Sat. VI, v, 459).

CHAPTER XV

OF THE PERILS OF HIS ABBEY AND OF THE REASONS
FOR THE WRITING OF THIS HIS LETTER

REFLECTING often upon all these things, I determined to make provision for those sisters and to undertake their care in every way I could. Furthermore, in order that they might have the greater reverence for me, I arranged to watch over them in person. And since now the persecution carried on by my sons was greater and more incessant than that which I formerly suffered at the hands of my brethren, I returned frequently to the nuns, fleeing the rage of the tempest as to a haven of peace. There, indeed, could I draw breath for a little in quiet, and among them my labours were fruitful, as they never were among the monks. All this was of the utmost benefit to me in body and soul, and it was equally essential for them by reason of their weakness.

But now has Satan beset me to such an extent that I no longer know where I may find rest, or even so much as live. I am driven hither and yon, a fugitive and a vagabond, even as the accursed Cain (Gen. iv, 14). I have already said that "without were fightings, within were fears" (II Cor. vii, 5), and these torture me ceaselessly, the fears being indeed without as well as within, and the fightings wheresoever there are fears. Nay, the persecution carried on by my sons rages against me more perilously and continuously than that of my open enemies, for my sons I have always with me, and I am ever exposed to their treacheries. The violence of my enemies I see in the danger to my body if I leave the cloister; but within it I am compelled incessantly to endure the crafty machinations as well as the open violence of those monks who are called my sons, and who are entrusted to me as their abbot, which is to say their father.

Oh, how often have they tried to kill me with poison, even as the monks sought to slay St. Benedict! Methinks the same reason which led the saint to abandon his wicked sons might encourage me to follow the example of so great a father, lest, in thus exposing myself to certain peril, I might be deemed a rash tempter of God rather than a lover of Him, nay, lest it might even be judged that I had thereby taken my own life. When I had safeguarded myself to the best of my ability, so far as my food and drink were concerned, against their daily plottings, they sought to destroy me in the very ceremony of the altar by putting poison in the chalice. One day, when I had gone to Nantes to visit the count, who was then sick, and while I was sojourning awhile in the house of one of my brothers in the flesh, they arranged to poison me, with the connivance of one of my attendants, believing that I would take no precautions to escape such a plot. But divine providence so ordered matters that I had no desire for the food which was set before me; one of the monks whom I had brought with me ate thereof, not knowing that which had been done, and straightway fell dead. As for the attendant who had dared to undertake this crime, he fled in terror alike of his own conscience and of the clear evidence of his guilt.

After this, as their wickedness was manifest to every one, I began openly in every way I could to avoid the danger with which their plots threatened me, even to the extent of leaving the abbey and dwelling with a few others apart in little cells. If the monks knew beforehand that I was going anywhere on a journey, they bribed bandits to waylay me on the road and kill me. And while I was struggling in the midst of these dangers, it chanced one day that the hand of the Lord smote me a heavy blow, for I fell from my horse, breaking a bone in my neck, the injury causing me greater pain and weakness than my former wound.

Using excommunication as my weapon to coerce the untamed rebelliousness of the monks, I forced certain ones among them whom I particularly feared to promise me publicly, pledging their faith or swearing upon the sacrament, that they would thereafter depart from the abbey and no longer trouble me in any way. Shamelessly and openly did they violate the pledges they had given and their sacramental oaths, but finally they were compelled to give this and many other promises under oath, in the presence of the count and the bishops, by the authority of the Pontiff of Rome, Innocent, who sent his own legate for this special purpose. And yet even this did not bring me peace. For when I returned to the abbey after the expulsion of those whom I have just mentioned, and entrusted myself to the remaining brethren, of whom I felt less suspicion, I found them even worse than the others. I barely succeeded in escaping them, with the aid of a certain nobleman of the district, for they were planning, not to poison me indeed, but to cut my throat with a sword. Even to the present time I stand face to face with this danger, fearing the sword which threatens my neck so that I can scarcely draw a free breath between one meal and the next. Even so do we read of him who, reckoning the power and heaped-up wealth of the tyrant Dionysius as a great blessing, beheld the sword secretly hanging by a hair above his head, and so learned what kind of happiness comes as the result of worldly power (Cicer. 5, Tusc.) Thus did I too learn by constant experience, I who had been exalted from the condition of a poor monk to the dignity of an abbot, that my wretchedness increased .with my wealth; and I would that the ambition of those who voluntarily seek such power might be curbed by my example.

And now, most dear brother in Christ and comrade closest to me in the intimacy of speech, it should suffice for your sorrows and the hardships you have endured that I have written this story of my own misfortunes, amid which I have toiled almost from the cradle. For so, as I said in the beginning of this letter, shall you come to regard your tribulation as nought, or at any rate as little, in comparison with mine, and so shall you bear it more lightly in measure as you regard it as less. Take comfort ever in the saying of Our Lord, what he foretold for his followers at the hands of the followers of the devil: "If they have persecuted me, they will also persecute you (John xv, 20). If the world hate you, ye know that it hated me before it hated you. If ye were of the world, the world would love his own" (ib. 18-19). And the apostle says: "All that will live godly in Christ Jesus shall suffer persecution" (II Tim. iii, 12). And elsewhere he says: "I do not seek to please men. For if I yet pleased men, I should not be the servant of Christ" (Galat. i, 10). And the Psalmist says: "They who have been pleasing to men have been confounded, for that God hath despised them."

Commenting on this, St. Jerome, whose heir methinks I am in the endurance of foul slander, says in his letter to Nepotanius: "The apostle says: 'If I yet pleased men, I should not be the servant of Christ.' He no longer seeks to please men, and so is made Christ's servant" (Epist. 2). And again, in his letter to Asella regarding those whom he was falsely accused of loving: "I give thanks to my God that I am worthy to be one whom the world hates" (Epist. 99). And to the monk Heliodorus he writes: "You are wrong, brother, you are wrong if you think there is ever a time when the Christian does not suffer persecution. For our adversary goes about as a roaring lion seeking what he may devour, and do you still think of peace? Nay, he lieth in ambush among the rich."

Inspired by those records and examples, we should endure our persecutions all the more steadfastly the more bitterly they harm us. We should not doubt that even if they are not according to our deserts, at least they serve for the purifying of our souls. And since all things are done in accordance with the divine ordering, let every one of true faith console himself amid all his afflictions with the thought that the great goodness of God permits nothing to be done without reason, and brings to a good end whatsoever may seem to happen wrongfully. Wherefore rightly do all men say: "Thy will be done." And great is the consolation to all lovers of God in the word of the Apostle when he says: "We know that all things work together for good to them that love God" (Rom. viii, 28). The wise man of old had this in mind when he said in his Proverbs: "There shall no evil happen to the just" (Prov. xii, 21). By this he clearly shows that whosoever grows wrathful for any reason against his sufferings has therein departed from the way of the just, because he may not doubt that these things have happened to him by divine dispensation. Even such are those who yield to their own rather than to the divine purpose, and with hidden desires resist the spirit which echoes in the words, "Thy will be done," thus placing their own will ahead of the will of God. Farewell.

Appendix

APPENDIX

Pierre Abélard

Petrus Abælardus (or Abailardus) was born in the year 1079 at Palets, a Breton town not far from Nantes. His father, Berengarius, was a nobleman of some local importance; his mother, Lucia, was likewise of noble family. The name "Abælardus" is said to be a corruption of "Habelardus," which, in turn, was substituted by himself for the nickname "Bajolardus" given to him in his student days. However the name may have arisen, the famous scholar certainly adopted it very early in his career, and it went over into the vernacular as "Abélard" or "Abailard," though with a multiplicity of variations (in Villon's famous poem, for example, it appears as "Esbaillart").

For the main facts of Abélard's life his own writings remain the best authority, but through his frequent contact with many of the foremost figures in the intellectual and clerical life of the early twelfth century it has been possible to check his own account of his career with considerable accuracy. The story told in the "Historia Calamitatum" covers the events of his life from boyhood to about 1132 or 1133, —in other words, up to approximately his fifty-third or fifty-fourth year. That the account he gives of himself is substantially correct cannot be doubted; making all due allow-

ance for the violence of his feelings, which certainly led him to colour many incidents in a manner unfavourable to his enemies, the main facts tally closely with all the external evidence now available.

A very brief summary of the events of the final years of his life will serve to round out the story. The "Historia Calamitatum" was written while Abélard was still abbot of the monastery of St. Gildas, in Brittany. The terrors of his existence there are fully dwelt on in his autobiographical letter, and finally, in 1134 or 1135, he fled, living for a short time in retirement. In 1136, however, we find him once more lecturing, and apparently with much of his former success, on Mont Ste. Geneviève. His old enemies were still on his trail, and most of all Bernard of Clairvaux, to whose fiery adherence to the faith Abélard's rationalism seemed a sheer desecration. The unceasing activities of Bernard and others finally brought Abélard before an ecclesiastical council at Sens in 1140, where he was formally arraigned on charges of heresy. Had Abélard's courage held good, he might have won his case, for Bernard was frankly terrified at the prospect of meeting so formidable a dialectitian, but Abélard, broken in spirit by the prolonged persecution from which he had suffered, contented himself with appealing to the Pope. The indefatigable Bernard at once proceeded to secure a condemnation of Abélard from Rome, whither the accused man set out to plead his case. On the way, however, he collapsed, both physically and in spirit, and remained for a few months at the abbey of Cluny, whence his friends removed him, a dying man, to the priory of St. Marcel, near Châlons-sur-Saône. Here he died on April 21, 1142.

A discussion of Abélard's position among the scholastic philosophers would necessarily go far beyond the proper limits of a mere historical note. He stands out less commandingly as a constructive philosopher than as a master of dialectics. He was, as even his enemies admitted, a brilliant teacher and an unconquerable logician; he was, moreover, a voluminous writer. Works by him which have been preserved include letters, sermons, philosophical and religious treatises, commentaries on the Bible, on Aristotle and on various other books, and a number of poems.

Many of the misfortunes which the "Historia Calamitatum" relates were the direct outcome of Abélard's uncompromising position as a rationalist, and the document is above all interesting for the picture it gives of the man himself, against the background of early twelfth century France. A few dates will help the general reader to connect the life surrounding Abélard with other and more familiar facts. William the Conqueror had entered England thirteen years before Abélard's birth. The boy was eight years old when the Conqueror died near Rouen during his struggle with Philip of France. He was seventeen when the First Crusade began, and twenty when the crusaders captured Jerusalem.

Two of the men who most profoundly influenced the times in which Abélard lived were Hildebrand, famous as Pope Gregory VII, and Louis VI (the Fat), king of France. It was to Hildebrand that the Church owed much of that regeneration of the spirit which gave it such vitality throughout the twelfth century. Hildebrand died, indeed, when Abélard was only six years old, but he left the Church such a force in the affairs of men as it had never been before. As for Louis the Fat, who reigned from 1108 to 1137, it was he who began to lift the royal power in France out of the shadow which the slothfulness and incompetence of his immediate predecessors, Henry I and Philip I, had cast over it. Discerning enough to see that the chief enemies of the crown were the great nobles, and constantly advised by a minister of exceptional wisdom, Suger, abbot of St. Denis, Louis did his utmost to protect the towns and the churches, and to bring that small part of France wherein his power was felt out of the anarchy and chaos of the eleventh century.

It was the France of Louis VI and Suger which formed the background for the great battle between the realists and the nominalists, the battle in which Abélard played no small part. His life was divided between the towns wherein he taught and the Church which alternately welcomed and denounced him. His fellow-disputants have their places in the history of philosophy; the story of Abélard's love for Héloïse has set him apart, so that he has lived for eight centuries less as a fearless thinker and masterly logician than as one of the glowingly romantic figures of the Middle Ages.

"A Friend"

It is not known to whom Abélard's letter was addressed, but it may be guessed that the writer intended it to reach the *hands of Héloïse. This actually happened, and the first and most famous letter from Héloïse to Abélard was substantially an answer to the "Historia Calamitatum."*

WILLIAM OF CHAMPEAUX

William of Champeaux (Gulielmus Campellensis) was born about 1070 at Champeaux, near Melun. He studied under Anselm of Laon and Roscellinus, his training in philosophy thereby being influenced by both realism and nominalism. His own inclination, however, was strongly towards the former, and it was as a determined proponent of realism that he began to teach in the school of the cathedral of Notre Dame, of which he was made canon in 1103. In 1108 he withdrew to the abbey of St. Victor, and subsequently became bishop of Châlons-sur-Marne. He died in 1121. As a teacher his influence was wide; he was a vigorous defender of orthodoxy and a passionate adversary of the heterodox philosophy of his former master, Roscellinus. That he and Abélard disagreed was only natural, but Abélard's statement that he argued William into abandoning the basic principles of his philosophy is certainly untrue.

"THE UNIVERSALS"

It is not within the province of such a note as this to discuss in detail the great controversy between the realists and the nominalists which dominated the philosophical and, to some extent, the religious thought of France during the first half of the twelfth century. In brief, the realists maintained that the idea is a reality distinct from and independent of

[85]

the individuals constituting it; their motto, Universalia sunt realia, *was readily capable of extension far beyond the Church, and William of Champeaux himself carried it to the extent of arguing that nothing is real but the universal. The nominalists, on the other hand, argued that "universals" are mere notions of the mind, and that individuals alone are real; their motto was* Universalia sunt nomina. *Thus the central question in the long controversy concerned the reality of abstract or incorporate ideas, and it is to be observed that the realists held views diametrically opposite to those which the word "realism" today implies. In upholding the reality of the idea, they were what would now be called idealists, whereas their opponents, denying the reality of abstractions and insisting on that of the concrete individual or object, were realists in the modern sense.*

The peculiar importance of this controversy lay in its effect on the status of the Church. If nominalism should prevail, then the Church would be shorn of much of its authority, for its greatest power lay in the conception of it as an enduring reality outside of and above all the individuals who shared in its work. It is not strange, then, that the ardent realism of William of Champeaux should have been outraged by the nominalistic logic of Abélard. Abélard, indeed, never went to such extreme lengths as the arch-nominalist, Roscellinus, who was duly condemned for heresy by the Council of Soissons in 1092, but he went quite far enough to win for himself the undying enmity of the leading realists, who were followed by the great majority of the clergy.

PORPHYRY

The Introduction ("Isagoge") to the Categories of Aristotle, written by the Greek scholar and neoplatonist Porphyry in the third century A. D., was translated into Latin by Boetius, and in this form was extensively used throughout the Middle Ages as a compendium of Aristotelian logic. As a philosopher Porphyry was chiefly important as the immediate successor of Plotinus in the neoplatonic school at Rome, but his "Isagoge" had extraordinary weight among the medieval logicians.

PRISCIAN

The Institutiones grammaticae *of Priscian (Priscianus Caesariensis) formed the standard grammatical and philological textbook of the Middle Ages, its importance being fairly indicated by the fact that today there exist about a thousand manuscript copies of it.*

ANSELM

Anselm of Laon was born somewhere about 1040, and is said to have studied under the famous St. Anselm, later archbishop of Canterbury, at the monastery of Bec. About 1070 he began to teach in Paris, where he was notably successful. Subsequently he returned to Laon, where his school of theology and exegetics became the most famous one in Europe. His most important work, an interlinear gloss on the Scriptures, was regarded as authoritative throughout the later Middle Ages. He died in 1117. That he was something of a pedant is probable, but Abélard's picture of him is certainly very far from doing him justice.

[87]

Of these two not much is known beyond what Abélard himself tells us. Alberic, indeed, won a considerable reputation, and was highly recommended to Pope Honorius II by St. Bernard. In 1139 Alberic seems to have become archbishop of Bourges, dying two years later. Lotulphe the Lombard is referred to by another authority as Leutaldus Novariensis.

ST. JEROME

The enormous scholarship of St. Jerome, born about 340 and dying September 30, 420, made him not only the foremost authority within the Church itself throughout the Middle Ages, but also one of the chief guides to secular scholarship. Abélard repeatedly quotes from him, particularly from his denunciation of the revival of Gnostic heresies by Jovinianus and from some of his voluminous epistles. He also refers extensively to the charges brought against Jerome by reason of his teaching of women at Rome in the house of Marcella. One of his pupils, Paula, a wealthy widow, followed him on his journey through Palestine, and built three nunneries at Bethlehem, of which she remained the head up to the time of her death in 404.

ST. AUGUSTINE

Regarding the position of St. Augustine (354-430) throughout the Middle Ages, it is here sufficient to quote a few words of Gustav Krüger: "The theological position and influence of Augustine may be said to be unrivalled. No single name has ever exercised such power over the Christian

Church, and no one mind ever made so deep an impression on Christian thought. In him scholastics and mystics, popes and opponents of the papal supremacy, have seen their champion. He was the fulcrum on which Luther rested the thoughts by which he sought to lift the past of the Church out of the rut; yet the judgment of Catholics still proclaims the ideals of Augustine as the only sound basis of philosophy."

ABBEY OF ST. DENIS

The abbey of St. Denis was founded about 625 by Dagobert, son of Lothair II, at some distance from the basilica which the clergy of Paris had erected in the fifth century over the saint's tomb. Long renowned as the place of burial for most of the kings of France, the abbey of St. Denis had a particular importance in Abélard's day by reason of its close association with the reigning monarch. The abbot to whom Abélard refers so bitterly was Adam of St. Denis, who began his rule of the monastery about 1094. In 1106 this same Adam chose as his secretary one of the inmates of the monastery, Suger, destined shortly to become the most influential man in France through his position as advisor to Louis VI, and also the foremost historian of his time. Adam died in 1123, and his successor, referred to by Abélard in Chapter X, was none other than Suger himself. From 1127 to 1137 Suger devoted most of his time to the reorganization and reform of the monastery of St. Denis. If we are to believe Abélard, such reform was sorely needed, but other contemporary evidence by no means fully sustains Abélard in his condemnation of Adam and his fellow monks.

[89]

ORIGEN

The Alexandrian theological writer Origen, who lived from about 185 to 254, was the most distinguished and the most influential of all the theologians of the ancient Church, with the single exception of Augustine. His incredible industry resulted in such a mass of writings that Jerome himself asked in despair, "Which of us can read all that he has written?" Origen's self-mutilation, referred to by Abélard, was subsequently used by his enemies as an argument for deposing him from his presbyterial status.

ATHANASIUS

Abélard's tract regarding the power of God to create Himself was one of the many distant echoes of the great Arian-Athanasian controversy of the fourth century. St. Athanasius, bishop of Alexandria, well deserved the title conferred on him by the Church as "the father of orthodoxy," and it was by his name that the doctrine of identity of substance ("the Son is of the same substance with the Father") became known. Much of the life of Athanasius was passed amid persecutions at the hands of his enemies, and on several occasions he was driven into exile.

RODOLPHE, ARCHBISHOP OF RHEIMS

Rodolphe, or, as some authorities call him, Rudolph or Radulph, became archbishop of Rheims in 1114, after having served as treasurer of the cathedral. His importance among the French clergy is attested by the many references to him in contemporary documents.

CONON OF PRAENESTE

Conon, bishop of Praeneste, whose real name may have been Conrad, came to France as papal legate on at least two occasions. He represented Paschal II in 1115 at ecclesiastical councils held in Beauvais, Rheims and Châlons; in 1120 he represented Calixtus II at Soissons on the occasion of Abélard's trial.

GEOFFROI OF CHARTRES

Geoffroi, bishop of Chartres, the second of the name to hold that post, was subsequently a warm friend of St. Bernard. Abélard's high estimate of him is fully confirmed by other contemporary authorities.

ABBOT OF ST. MÉDARD

This abbot was probably, though not certainly, Anselm of Soissons, who became a bishop in 1145. The chronology, however, is confusing.

DIONYSIUS THE AREOPAGITE

The confusion regarding the identity of Dionysius the Areopagite persists to this day, at least to the extent that we do not know the real name of the fourth or fifth century writer who, under this pseudonym, exercised so profound an influence on medieval thought. That he was not the bishop of either Athens or Corinth, nor yet the Dionysius who became the patron saint of France, is clear enough. Of the actual Dionysius the Areopagite we know practically nothing. He is mentioned in Acts, xvii, 34, as one of those Athe-

nians who believed when they had heard Paul preach on Mars Hill. A century or more later we learn from another Dionysius, bishop of Corinth, that Dionysius the Areopagite was the first bishop of Athens, a statement of doubtful value. In the fourth or fifth century a Greek theological writer of extraordinary erudition assumed the name of Dionysius the Areopagite, and as his works exerted an enormous influence on later scholarship, it was quite natural that the personal legend of the real Dionysius should have been extended correspondingly.

The Hilduin referred to by Abélard, who was abbot of St. Denis from 814 to 840, was directly responsible for the extreme phase of this extension. Accepting, as most of his contemporaries unquestioningly did, the identity of the theological writer with the Dionysius mentioned in Acts and spoken of as bishop of Athens, Hilduin went one step further, and demonstrated that this Dionysius was likewise the Dionysius (Denis) who had been sent into Gaul and martyred at Catulliacus, the modern St. Denis. There is no evidence to support Hilduin's contention, and the chronology of Gregory of Tours is quite sufficient to disprove it, but none the less it was enthusiastically accepted in France, and above all by the monks of St. Denis.

There was, however, a persistent doubt as to the identity of the Dionysius whose writings had become so famous. Bede, the authority quoted by Abélard, was, of course, wrong in saying that he was the bishop of Corinth, but anything which tended to shake the triple identity, established by Hildui_r, of the Dionysius of Athens who listened to St. Paul, of the pseudo-Areopagite whose works were known to every medieval scholar, and of the St. Denis who had become the patron saint of France, was naturally anathematized by the monks who bore the saint's name. Bede and Abélard were by no means accurate, but Bede's inkling of the truth was quite enough to get Abélard into serious trouble.

Theobald of Champagne

Theobald II, Count of Blois, Meaux and Champagne, was one of the most powerful nobles in France, and by the extent of his influence fully deserved the title of "the Great" by which he was subsequently known. His domain included the modern departments of Ardennes, Marne, Aube and Haute-Marne, with part of Aisne, Seine-et-Marne, Yonne and Meuse. Furthermore, his mother Adela, was the daughter of William I of England, and his younger brother, Stephen, was King of England from 1135 to 1154. Theobald became Count of Blois in 1102, Count of Champagne in 1125, and Count of Troyes in 1128. Had he so chosen, he might likewise have become Duke of Normandy after the death of his uncle, Henry I of England, in 1135. He died in 1152.

Stephen the Seneschal

There is much doubt as to whether this Stephen was Stephen de Garland, dapifer, or another Stephen, who was royal chancellor under Louis the Fat. A charter of the year 1124 is signed by both Stephen dapifer and Stephen cancellarius. *Probably, however, the authority identifying Stephen* dapifer *as Stephen de Garland, seneschal of France, is trustworthy.*

THE PARACLETE

Among the terms which are characteristic of, or even peculiar to, the Gospel of St. John is that of "the Paraclete," rendered in the King James version "the Comforter." The Greek word of which "Paraclete" is a reproduction literally means "advocate," one called to aid; hence "intercessor." The doctrine of the Paraclete appears chiefly in John, xiv and xv. For example: (xiv, 16-17) "And I will pray the Father, and he shall give you another Comforter (Paraclete) that he may abide with you for ever; even the spirit of truth." Again: (xiv, 26) "But the Comforter (Paraclete), which is the Holy Ghost, whom the Father will send in my name, he shall teach you all things." With John's words as a basis, the Paraclete came to be regarded as identical with the Third Person of the Trinity, but always with the special attributes of consolation and intercession.

NORBERT OF PRÉMONTRÉ

In 1120 there was established at Prémontré, a desert place in the diocese of Laon, a monastery of canons regular who followed the so-called Rule of St. Augustine, but with supplementary statutes which made the life one of exceptional severity. The head of this monastery was Norbert, subsequently canonized. His order received papal approbation in 1126, and thereafter it spread rapidly throughout Europe;

two hundred years later there were no less than seventeen hundred Norbertine or Premonstratensian monasteries. Norbert himself became archbishop of Magdeburg, and it was in Germany that the most notable work of his order was accomplished.

BERNARD OF CLAIRVAUX

Regarding the illustrious St. Bernard, abbot of Clairvaux, it is needless here to say more than that his own age recognized in him the embodiment of the highest ideal of medieval monasticism. Intellectually inferior to Abélard and to some others of those over whom he triumphed, he was their superior in moral strength, in zeal, and above all in the power of making others share his own enthusiasms. Born in 1090, he was renowned as one of the foremost of French churchmen before he was thirty years old; his share in the contest which followed the death of Pope Honorius II in 1130 made him one of the most commanding figures in all Europe. It was to him that the Cistercian order owed its extraordinary expansion in the twelfth century. That Abélard should have fallen before so redoubtable an adversary (see the note on Pierre Abélard) is in no way surprising, but there can be no doubt that St. Bernard's "persecution" of Abélard was inspired solely by high ideals and an intense zeal for the truth as Bernard perceived it.

ABBEY OF ST. GILDAS

Traditionally, at least, this abbey was the oldest one in Brittany. According to the anonymous author of the Life *and Deeds of St. Gildas, it was founded during the reign of Childeric, the second of the Merovingian kings, in the fifth century. Be that as it may, its authentic history had been extensive before Abélard assumed the direction of its affairs. His gruesome picture of the conditions which prevailed there cannot, of course, be accepted as wholly accurate, but even allowing for gross exaggeration, the life of the monks must have been quite sufficiently scandalous. It was apparently in the closing period of Abélard's sojourn at the abbey of St. Gildas that he wrote the "Historia Calamitatum." He endured the life there for nearly ten years; the date of his flight is not certain, but it cannot have been far from 1134 or 1135.*

Leo IX

Leo IX, pope from 1049 to 1054, was a native of Upper Alsace. It was at the Easter synod of 1049 that he enjoined anew the celibacy of the clergy, in connection with which the letter quoted by Abélard was written.